U.S. History Matters

A Student Guide to U.S. History Online

U.S. History Matters

A Student Guide to U.S. History Online

SECOND EDITION

Kelly Schrum
Alan Gevinson
Roy Rosenzweig

George Mason University

Bedford/St. Martin's

Boston ◆ New York

For Bedford/St. Martin's

Publisher for History: Mary Dougherty
Director of Development for History: Jane Knetzger
Developmental Editor: Louise Townsend
Production Editor: Lindsay DiGianvittorio
Senior Production Supervisor: Dennis J. Conroy
Executive Marketing Manager: Jenna Bookin Barry
Copyeditor: Steven M. Patterson
Text Design: Lisa Buckley Design
Cover Design: Sara Gates
Composition: Achorn International, Inc.
Printing and Binding: Haddon Craftsman, Inc., an RR Donnelley & Sons Company

President: Joan E. Feinberg
Editorial Director: Denise B. Wydra
Director of Marketing: Karen R. Soeltz
Director of Editing, Design, and Production: Marcia Cohen
Assistant Director of Editing, Design, and Production: Elise S. Kaiser
Managing Editor: Elizabeth M. Schaaf

Library of Congress Control Number: 2008937679

Manufactured in the United States of America.

3 2 1 0 9 8
f e d c b a

For information, write: Bedford/St. Martin's, 75 Arlington Street, Boston, MA 02116
(617-399-4000)

ISBN-10: 0–312–47838–0
ISBN-13: 978–0–312–47838–4

At the time of publication all Internet URLs published in this text were found to accurately link to their intended Web site. If you find a broken link, please forward the information to history@bedfordstmartins.com so that it can be corrected for the next printing.

Dedication

We dedicate this book to Roy Rosenzweig (1950–2007),
founder of the Center for History and New Media,
leader and visionary in the field of digital humanities,
and devoted friend and mentor.

Preface

In the twenty-first century, the Internet is ubiquitous, an integral part of our daily lives. We communicate, work, check news, traffic, and weather, and play online. It is also a powerful tool for learning and researching history. Little more than a decade ago, the Web offered limited access to serious historical scholarship and primary source archives. A search on a central figure in American history, such as Thomas Jefferson, likely yielded fewer than one hundred hits. Today, a *Google* search on "Thomas Jefferson" returns more than 13 million results, from a *Wikipedia* entry to tens of thousands of Jefferson documents, including political writings and speeches, correspondence, and financial books, not to mention thousands of quotes from this founding father, a virtual tour of his home at Monticello, and an academic discussion of his relationship with Sally Hemmings.

There are now hundreds of millions of primary sources available online for studying the past, as well as reliable and accessible secondary sources. The very abundance of the offerings, however, creates new challenges. Students and teachers continually ask, How do I find valuable materials? How can I quickly identify resources that will help me with a specific topic? How do I avoid misleading and even fraudulent documents? *U.S. History Matters*, Second Edition, provides a solution, offering a safe path through the overwhelming mass of historical sources and interpretations available online by providing an annotated guide to exemplary websites for the study of U.S. history. The guide is selective rather than comprehensive, highlighting 250 websites that present a compelling and broad range of resources for studying themes or special topics throughout the American past. It emphasizes collections of primary sources with the goal of helping students learn to conduct historical research and quickly locate reliable websites for doing so.

Content and Organization

U.S. History Matters opens with a revised and expanded introduction to history research online, emphasizing valuable resources, potential pitfalls (and how to avoid them), and guidance for working with online primary and secondary sources, from how to tell them apart to how to analyze them. The new introduction presents strategies for navigating the Web as well as making the most of Web 2.0 resources, discussing the recent explosion of collaborative and participatory websites such as wikis and YouTube and their impact on historical research. Plagiarism is especially prevalent in the online era, and our section titled "A Word About Plagiarism" provides tips to help students understand and avoid it, followed by a guide to citing online resources.

The remainder of the volume is devoted to the 250 carefully chosen and annotated U.S. history websites, drawn from *History Matters: The U.S. Survey*

Course on the Web, **http://historymatters.gmu.edu**, a collaborative project developed by the Center for History and New Media (CHNM) at George Mason University and the American Social History Project/Center for Media and Learning (ASHP/CML) at the Graduate Center, City University of New York. *History Matters* offers more than a thousand website reviews from which the 250 for this guide have been culled. The list begins with a section "General Websites for U.S. History Research" that presents websites addressing themes throughout U.S. history or across multiple time periods. The remaining annotations are organized into nine conventional chronological divisions to reflect how most students study U.S. history. The website annotations, drawn from longer reviews on the *History Matters* website, are relatively short by design. They provide a snapshot of each website—a sense of its strengths and weaknesses, a brief summary of the resources available, and its general approach. (We encourage you to visit *History Matters* for longer reviews and additional resources.)

This second edition contains 25 percent new websites, offering expanded coverage of important topics and a stronger emphasis on multimedia materials. We have doubled the number of websites on Native American history, have included more sites pertaining to the history of women and gender, and offer more websites that feature *varieties* of primary sources such as audio and video clips, maps, and different kinds of illustrations, such as advertisements. Newly redesigned icons allow students to quickly identify those websites that contain primary documents, images, and audio, video, map, and statistical resources, as well as which sites require a subscription. The book closes with a set of helpful appendices—a "Glossary of Common Internet Terms," an alphabetical list of the websites reviewed, and an index of topics, sources, and regions.

The Internet now offers an abundance of quality online materials unavailable even a decade ago, and we hope this guide will prove a valuable resource to students in navigating many of these sites. It is important to remember that vast quantities of primary sources, such as diaries, films, and manuscript collections, are not available digitally and may never be, and that secondary sources are often most easily available in print in the library. But given the riches available online, this book is intended as a guide to navigating them wisely and efficiently, as well as learning how to study the context and content of the sources and topics in question. The most important way to become an intelligent consumer of historical resources online is to become a good historian by learning to use and apply the skills of critical analysis that historians rely upon.

Note to Teachers: Teaching Resources Available on the *History Matters* Website

The *History Matters* website, **http://historymatters.gmu.edu**, offers additional resources for teaching U.S. history. One resource includes a set of longer website reviews, co-published with the *Journal of American History* and available online at **http://historymatters.gmu.edu/browse/wwwhistory**. Each review offers in-depth analysis of a specific website, and many provide specific teaching suggestions. For example, Daniel Pope's review of *Emergence of Advertising in America: 1850–1920* [122], **http://library.duke.edu/digitalcollections/eaa/**, explores the many strengths of the website's resources and suggests areas ripe for study, such as comparing illustrations of children in advertising from 1880 to 1910. Pope also raises important issues concerning the fragmentary nature of advertisements studied in isolation and poses questions such as how and where advertisements were presented and how consumers reacted.

Another valuable teaching resource on the *History Matters* website is *Making Sense of Evidence*, **http://historymatters.gmu.edu/browse/makesense**, a series of guides to analyzing different kinds of primary sources such as advertisements, maps, photographs, and diaries. These eight written guides and eight multimedia presentations pose questions specific to each kind of source, such as who is conducting the interview in an oral history and what popular songs can tell us about American society. They also model the processes scholars use to make sense of sources: visitors can listen to historian Larry Levine analyze a 1930s blues song recorded in a Texas prison, or watch museum curator Barbara Clark Smith discuss a colonial era newspaper article on a 1775 political demonstration in Providence, Rhode Island. These guides provide an excellent starting point for helping students wisely venture down the path of historical thinking and primary source analysis.

Acknowledgments

As mentioned above, *U.S. History Matters*, Second Edition, is based on the *History Matters* website which was initially developed by Pennee Bender, Steven Brier, Joshua Brown, and Roy Rosenzweig. They were later joined by Ellen Noonan and Kelly Schrum. We want to thank our colleagues on the *History Matters* team as well as our funders—the National Endowment for the Humanities, The Kellogg Foundation, The Rockefeller Foundation, George Mason University, the Virginia Foundation for the Humanities, City University of New York, and the New York Council for the Humanities—for making this work possible.

We are grateful for the valuable feedback from reviewers of the first edition of *History Matters* and thank them for their helpful comments, insights, and suggestions for this second edition: S. Max Edelson, University of Illinois, Urbana-Champaign; Victoria Getis, The Ohio State University; Charlene Boyer Lewis, Kalamazoo College; Steven Noll, University of Florida, Gainesville; G. David Price, Santa Fe Community College; Sandra Schackel, Boise State University; Douglas Seefeldt, University of Nebraska–Lincoln; and Laura Trauth, Community College of Baltimore County.

The 250 website annotations in this book are based on the more than one thousand annotations written for the website over many years. The authors of these original annotations include Laura Beveridge, Megan Elias, Alan Gevinson, Katharina Hering, Ben Huggins, Michael Laine, Kristin Lehner, Wendi Manuel-Scott, Michael O'Malley, Ellen Pearson, Elena Razlogova, Roy Rosenzweig, Kelly Schrum, and John Summers. Additional thanks are due to the research assistants at George Mason University who helped with the research, images, and preparation of this manuscript: Kristin Lehner, Meredith Mayo, Jennifer Reeder, Ammon Shepherd, Arminda Smith, and Amanda Shuman. Finally, we want to express our appreciation to publishers Joan Feinberg, Mary Dougherty, Jane Knetzger, Kathryn Abbott, Louise Townsend, Katherine Flynn, and Lindsay DiGianvittorio at Bedford/St. Martin's who helped envision and shape this book.

Contents

U.S. History Matters

A Student Guide to U.S. History Online

1

An Introduction to
U.S. History Research Online

The Internet has become the largest and most diverse repository of historical primary sources in the world. Millions of resources covering almost any subject of historical inquiry are readily available and can be used to examine the complexities of the past across time and space. You can explore European perspectives of the New World without leaving your computer by visiting the *Archive of Early American Images* [56] website and viewing fifteenth- and sixteenth-century maps of the Americas (Fig. 1). Or enter the Salem, Massachusetts, courtroom in 1692 via the *Salem Witch Trials: Documentary Archive and Transcription Project* [66] that provides full-text versions of the three-volume, verbatim witch trial transcripts, as well as a host of related narratives, pamphlets, and sermons. You can listen to President Roosevelt ask Congress to declare war on Japan on December 8, 1941, at the *Franklin D. Roosevelt Presidential Library and Digital Archives* [195], a website offering 10,000 documents pertaining to Roosevelt's presidency,

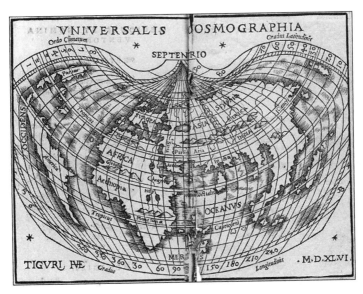

Fig. 1 Map, Spanish America, *Vniversalis cosmographia*, 1546 [56]. *(The John Carter Brown Library at Brown University.)*

including formerly classified correspondence, reports, and memoranda, as well as images and audio clips.

Perhaps your research topic centers on the lives of African Americans in the United States before and after the Civil War. You could visit websites on slavery, abolition, legal history, and popular culture, such as *Uncle Tom's Cabin and American Culture* [106], *Historical* New York Times *Project—The Civil War Years, 1860–1866* [102], or the *Freedmen's Bureau Online* [101]. Or maybe you were asked to discuss how artifacts of women's lives from the first half of the twentieth century fit into larger themes in U.S. history. Materials from *Votes for Women: Selections from the National American Woman Suffrage Association Collection, 1848–1921* [137] could be used to investigate political activism and changing roles of women, as could resources from the *Margaret Sanger Papers Project* [164] (Fig. 2) or the *Emma Goldman Papers* [154]. You could examine photographs of Zora Neale Hurston at the *Florida State Archives Photographic Collection* [19] or view advertisements reflecting the rise of a highly gendered consumer market at *Ad*Access* [185].

We now experience the Internet as a vast, rich, and primarily free library. Not all websites are created equal, though, and the resources available online are, at best, uneven in quality. A *Yahoo*, **http://www.yahoo.com**, search on "U.S. history" returns more than 1.5 billion results, led by **http://www.SuperDeluxe .com**, a Turner Broadcasting System website of original comedy video clips with no relation to United States history, and **http://www.MyCreditSearch.info**. A *Google* search on "colonial American history" also yields more than 1.5 million results, including syllabi, textbooks, and hotels located close to historic sites such as Colonial Williamsburg. So how do you wade through this enormous and sometimes confusing online world to find reliable information and resources? How can you avoid advertisements or personal pages with questionable stan-

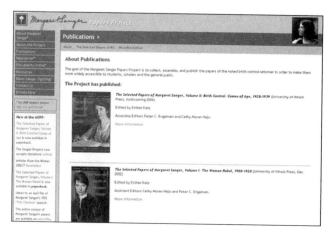

Fig. 2 Screenshot from *Margaret Sanger Papers Project* [164].
(Reprinted by permission of the Margaret Sanger Papers, New York University.)

Fig. 3 Page from Martha Ballard's diary, *Do History: Martha Ballard's Diary Online* [71]. *(Diary entry, Martha Ballard, April 9–16, 1785. Do History (http://dohistory.org). Reprinted with permission from the Center for History and New Media, George Mason University.)*

dards of historical analysis? Being web savvy does not automatically translate into critical use of online resources.

While the Web can offer valuable U.S. history material previously unavailable to most students, it can also be the purveyor of misinformation, poorly excerpted texts, or biased narratives. Online coverage of U.S. history crosses a broad range of regions, topics, and time periods, but is far from even or complete. For example, there are more websites covering topics in the late nineteenth and early twentieth centuries than there are with materials in the pre-colonial era. This is due, in part, to access and availability of materials. Copyright legislation also plays a role. Materials created before 1923 fall into the public domain and can be digitized and shared; materials created later in the twentieth century are restricted. So materials from the late nineteenth and early twentieth centuries are often more freely available than those in more recent decades. It is relatively easy to find online photographs, newspapers, and personal accounts for studying U.S. history; it is more challenging to find archaeology, music, or quantitative evidence. A wealth of websites address Native Americans, family life, popular culture, and military history, while fewer deal with Latinos, the environment, or the history of sexuality.

Numbers alone, however, do not tell the whole story. The key is finding quality materials that relate to your specific theme or topic. If you are researching women's history, you will find a wealth of resources within the subscription-based Alexander Street Press [2] website *North American Women's Letters and Diaries: Colonial to 1950*. This resource provides full-text letters and diaries from more than 1,000 women—totaling more than 21,000 documents and approximately 120,000 pages. If you are interested specifically in the medicinal practices of women in colonial America, however, *Do History: Martha Ballard's Diary Online* [71] presents the entire diary of eighteenth-century midwife Martha Ballard as handwritten pages and in transcription (Fig. 3), as well as a host of resources and tools for understanding Ballard's diary within the context of her world. Depending on the course and the project, a smaller website like this one may prove more valuable.

To help you find the best websites for your project, *History Matters* provides a roadmap for locating reliable sources quickly as well as a series of important questions to ask when you find them. Whatever your assignment or research topic, you are sure to find interesting and relevant resources awaiting further exploration.

Evaluating Websites

One of the greatest strengths of the Internet is its egalitarianism—anyone can post anything online. When it comes to historical research, this egalitarianism is both a strength and a weakness. On the positive side, it means that a rich, diverse pool of historical primary sources is widely available. On the negative side, far too many websites containing primary sources are of questionable quality. This situation places more responsibility on you, the user. There are several essential questions to ask when assessing a website's reliability—questions you need to answer before you start to use the primary sources found within.

Who Created the Website?

There is some basic information you should look for when you first visit a history website, starting with the author. Who created the website? Who wrote, gathered, or posted the materials presented? Sometimes this is straightforward, as you can see in this screenshot of the American Memory Project (Library of Congress) collection, *The African-American Experience in Ohio, 1850–1920* [110] (Fig. 4).

Fig. 4 Screenshot from *The African-American Experience in Ohio, 1850–1920* [110]. *(Courtesy of the Ohio Historical Society.)*

This website prominently displays its affiliation with the Library of Congress, as well as with the Ohio Historical Society, the organization that provided the materials for digitization. "American Memory" identifies the website as part of a rich body of digital primary source materials relating to the history and culture of the United States, including the papers of George Washington [76] and Abraham Lincoln [98], Civil War photographs [104], early motion pictures [140], and music and stories collected from many parts of the country [117, 120, 174, 203, 207].

Information concerning a website's author or creator is particularly important when the website presents historical interpretation. A good researcher will try to determine the point of view of the author and then evaluate how that perspective might affect the interpretation of sources presented. For example, conservative and liberal scholars would likely view the presidencies of Richard Nixon or William Clinton differently, just as Israelis and Palestinians likely interpret the history of the Middle East from different perspectives. Point of view can also affect online collections of primary sources since someone strongly committed to one interpretation of the past might select primary sources that largely support that position.

A related question is, Who hosts or publishes the website? Sometimes an "About," "Credits," or "Background" page offers information on who created or sponsors a website and why. An email address or contact information may provide clues as well. Knowing the affiliation of a website's author can help determine the reputability of a source. Is the author, webmaster, or main contact affiliated with a museum, library, or college?

If you do not find any useful information this way, you can try shortening the URL (Uniform Resource Locator). Start by removing the last characters of the URL, stopping before each forward slash (/), and pressing ENTER. If you receive an error page, remove another section of the URL. Sometimes this takes you to a larger subheading within a project. For example, material located at http://www.gwu.edu/~nsarchiv/NSAEBB/NSAEBB103/index.htm offers documentation of the efforts of President John F. Kennedy, shortly before his assassination, to establish a dialogue with Cuban President Fidel Castro. The materials are presented by the *National Security Archive*, a non-governmental institution that publishes declassified government materials. If you remove "index.htm," you find yourself on the same page. Removing the next section of the URL leaves you with http://www.gwu.edu/~nsarchiv/NSAEBB, a webpage that presents a list of all "Electronic Briefing Books" offered by the National Security Archive. Truncating once more to http://www.gwu.edu/~nsarchiv leads to the project's homepage where you can click "About" to learn more about the website's creator, host, and purpose.

> The National Security Archive is an independent non-governmental research institute and library located at The George Washington University in Washington, D.C. The Archive collects and publishes declassified documents acquired through the Freedom of Information Act (FOIA).[1]

[1]Thomas S. Blanton, National Security Archive, http://www.gwu.edu/~nsarchiv/nsa/the_archive.html (accessed December 18, 2007).

Not all URLs work this way. To present vast quantities of material, website creators increasingly use databases to organize their resources. This structure has many advantages, often making it easier to search the full text of documents and to access specific evidence, but it can result in URLs that are long and may not be permanent. In some cases, unwieldy URLs make it difficult to cite and share valuable resources. For example, this URL appears when you read *The Ballot and the Bullet*, a publication compiled by Carrie Chapman Catt in 1897 to challenge the claim that women should not be allowed to vote because they did not serve in the military:

> http://memory.loc.gov/cgi-bin/query/r?ammem/naw:@field+(SOURCE+@band
> (rbnawsa+n2415)):@@@REF

The URL is complicated and would be difficult to retype. To share the resource or locate the book at a later date, you may need to reference the main webpage that offers this material, *Votes for Women: Selections from the National American Woman Suffrage Association Collection, 1848–1921* [137], http://memory.loc.gov/ammem/naw/nawshome.html, and browse or search by title (*The Ballot and the Bullet*) or author (Carrie Chapman Catt) (Fig. 5).

In contrast, the *Avalon Project* [8], a collection of more than 600 full-text documents in law, history, economics, politics, diplomacy, and government, offers static webpages, pages not generated by a database, with permanent URLs. For example, you can read the *Mutual Defense Treaty Between the United States and the Republic of Korea* (1953) at http://www.yale.edu/lawweb/avalon/diplomacy/korea/kor001.htm. This structure also offers advantages and disadvantages. It may mean that the full text of the documents is not searchable as it would be with a database. On the other hand, the URL in this case offers information about the creator as well as the location of the document within the project under the headings "Diplomacy" and "Korea."

Shortening the URL to http://www.yale.edu/lawweb/avalon/diplomacy/korea or to http://www.yale.edu/lawweb/avalon/diplomacy does not reveal anything about the website's creator, but shortening a bit further takes you to the main page of the *Avalon Project*, http://www.yale.edu/lawweb/avalon. Shorten again, and you find the Yale University School of Law, the website's sponsor. If you remove "lawweb," you reach the Yale University homepage.

Yale University and its School of Law are well-respected institutions that lend credibility to the *Avalon Project* and the material it provides. Not every URL that ends in "*yale.edu*," however, is necessarily officially sanctioned by Yale University. Students and faculty often have access to URLs that include an institutional name. So http://www.ucla.edu/~jones might be the URL for someone named Jones who is affiliated with University of California at Los Angeles, but this does not equal an official university website. The *Alger Hiss Story* is a good example. The URL http://homepages.nyu.edu/~th15 identifies New York University as the host server. If you truncate the URL to http://homepages.nyu.edu, though, you find the following, strongly worded disclaimer, "Welcome to the home of the personal pages of faculty, staff, and students of NYU. These pages do not in any way con-

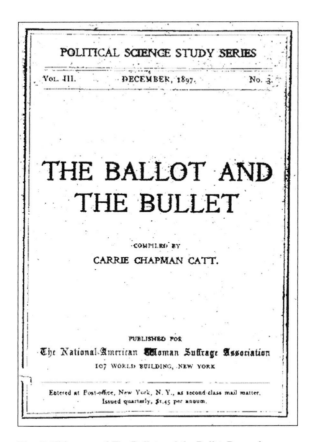

Fig. 5 Title page of *The Ballot and the Bullet*, December 1897, from *Votes for Women: Selections from the National American Woman Suffrage Association Collection, 1848–1921* [137]. *(Library of Congress, Rare Book and Special Collections Division, National American Woman Suffrage Association Collection.)*

stitute official New York University content. The views and opinions expressed in the pages are strictly those of the page authors, and comments on the contents of those pages should be directed to the page authors."[2]

To identify personal pages hosted on large institutional servers, you can look for personal names, a tilde (~), or words such as "home," "user," or "people." Commercial servers, such as *AOL*, *Yahoo*, and *Geocities*, also host many personal websites. On these servers, there are no definite rules regarding author and content quality. Some personal pages provide valuable historical resources, and at the same time, websites designed or hosted by large institutions sometimes offer flawed or incomplete information. A good researcher will approach all websites with skepticism and ask questions about why this material is available and who

[2]Homepages, New York University, **http://homepages.nyu.edu/** (accessed December 18, 2007).

funded and created the website. As a rule of thumb, though, websites created by museums, libraries, and colleges are created to present historical resources for educational purposes. Personal websites are often created to share an individual's passion for a certain topic and may or may not offer credible content.

Once upon a time in the history of the Internet it was possible to make some judgments about a website based upon its domain name. URLs issued in the United States that ended in *.com* signified commercial purposes, those ending in *.org* were intended for non-commercial purposes, and those ending in *.net* were intended for network providers. Today, however, any organization or individual can purchase a *.com, .net, .org, .biz, .tv,* or *.us* domain name, so these suffixes do not necessarily indicate who is responsible for a website. Outside the United States, domain names end with a two-letter code signifying the country where the website is based—or at least where the domain name was sold. Thus, an address ending in *.uk* is based in the United Kingdom and one ending in *.ch* is based in Switzerland. The exceptions to this free market in domain names are those based in the United States that are reserved for specific uses: *.edu* for educational institutions in the United States; *.mil* for the U.S. military; and *.gov* for the U.S. government. So, for instance, websites based at American colleges, universities, and schools all end in *.edu* and those at government institutions, such as the Department of State or National Archives, end in *.gov*.

Where Did the Sources on the Website Come From?

The next important question to ask is about the origin of the materials provided. The website *Geography of Slavery in Virginia* [75], created by the Virginia Center for Digital History and Thomas Costa at the University of Virginia College at Wise, offers transcriptions and images of more than 4,000 newspaper advertisements for runaway slaves and indentured servants between 1736 and 1803. The "About" page clearly states that this collection includes transcriptions and images of "all runaway and captured ads for slaves and servants placed in Virginia newspapers from 1736 to 1790," providing key information on the scope of the collection and the kind of information available. In addition, the full source information is provided making further research possible. For example, if you are especially interested in the advertisement for a slave named "Lewis" who was rumored to have "enlisted as a soldier," you could seek out the newspaper (*Virginia Gazette*) on microfilm for that particular day (July 12, 1780), and study the advertisement in its original context.

How Current Is the Website?

Information about when a website was created or updated can also be a valuable indicator of a website's reliability, although an archive of primary sources need not be updated frequently to remain useful. The website *Indian Affairs: Laws and Treaties* [29], created by the Oklahoma University Library between 1996 and 2000, offers the digitized contents of a seven-volume collection of treaties, laws, and executive orders relating to U.S.-Indian affairs. This website provides a fixed set of historical materials so it does not need to be edited or updated on a regular basis.

Websites that provide links to online resources, however, do require regular updating. The Kingwood College Library, for example, hosts a website named *American Cultural History, 1960–1969*, http://kclibrary.nhmccd.edu/decade60 .html. Created by reference librarians, the website offers links to other websites and primary sources related to major events, individuals, and cultural developments of the 1960s. Brief essays help contextualize specific trends in art, film, books, fashion, and music, but many of these links are no longer functional. A useful concept and once a valuable resource, in its present state this website is not the best place to find high-quality materials quickly.

Does the Website Present a Particular Perspective, Bias, or Agenda?

Content can also be revealing. What is the purpose of the website? Does it present facts or opinions? Does it have a particular bias or point of view? An openly biased website can still provide useful information, but it is most valuable when it clearly identifies its goals and distinguishes between fact and opinion. Is there a clear presentation or selection of materials? Is the website selling something?

There are more than one hundred websites sponsored by or affiliated with the Public Broadcasting Service (PBS) that cover topics in U.S. history, from medicine in early America to Tupperware to Jimmy Carter's presidency. PBS is a trusted source for reliable information, but many of these websites are created to promote PBS videos and offer little of historical significance beyond a description of the videos, a timeline, and classroom discussion questions. The *American Experience: Hawaii's Last Queen* is a good example, offering only these basics plus a quiz and a bibliography.[3]

A small number of PBS websites, however, offer a wealth of primary sources and tools for historical analysis. *Africans in America* [1], http://www.pbs.org/wgbh/ aia, for example, created as a companion to the television series of the same name, traces the history of Africans in America from the fifteenth-century slave trade to the Civil War (Fig. 6). The website offers close to 300 primary documents, including images and maps. Knowing that an online resource is hosted or created by PBS lends credibility, but does not provide enough information about the depth and content of the website. Further investigation is needed to determine if the material offered is valuable for historical research.

Other questions include intended audience and purpose. The answers can provide insight into whether or not a website is appropriate for your project. The *Philip Morris Advertising Archive*, created by Philip Morris Incorporated, provides a good example. Created as part of the Master Settlement Agreement with the tobacco industry, this website offers more than 55,000 color images of

---

[3]PBS, *American Experience: Hawaii's Last Queen*, http://www.pbs.org/wgbh/amex/hawaii (accessed December 20, 2007).

Fig. 6 Screenshot from *Africans in America* [1]. *(From the WGBH Educational Foundation. Copyright © 1998 WGBH/Boston.)*

tobacco advertisements, dating back to 1909. It is part of a larger online resource that offers more than 26 million pages of documents on the research, manufacturing, marketing, and sale of cigarettes from four tobacco companies and two industry organizations. The website presents an unparalleled amount of material for researching tobacco and cigarettes in American life, yet the search engine is confusing and materials are difficult to access. The settlement agreement mandated that companies make this information available, but did not require a user-friendly format.[4]

Who Else Considers This a Reliable Website?

Considering all of these factors will help provide a good sense of the quality of a website and the materials it presents. An additional way to assess the reliability of a website is to investigate its reputation. Which other websites and organizations find it valuable? Run a "link check" with *Google* by typing "link" and the complete URL into the *Google* search field as follows:

link:http://www.law.umkc.edu/faculty/projects/ftrials/ftrials.htm

This link check on *Famous Trials* [18], a project created by University of Missouri-Kansas City Law Professor Douglas Linder, returns 321 results. More than 300 websites link directly to this archive. Even more promising, many of these links come from library, teaching, and university websites, indicating that an academic

---

[4]Philip Morris Incorporated, *Philip Morris Advertising Archive*, **http://www.pmadarchive.com** (accessed December 18, 2007).

audience has favorably reviewed these materials. You can also look for reviews of a website in web or print publications that research and evaluate websites for educational use, such as the *Merlot Project*, http://www.merlot.org; the *Scout Report*, http://scout.wisc.edu; or the website *History Matters* [24].[5]

Web 2.0

Now that we have covered the main questions to ask as you evaluate historical resources online, we want to discuss two recent developments in digital history related to Web 2.0. Web 2.0 refers to a new generation of web applications, such as wikis and social-networking websites, that encourage collaboration and active participation among users. Web 2.0 developments impact history classrooms and historical research in many ways, and as with the Internet in general, are most valuable when we understand and assess their strengths and weaknesses.

The first development is the advent of websites based on *wiki* technologies. Wikis (the word comes from the Polynesian phrase *wiki-wiki* or *quick-quick*) are software platforms that allow anyone to add or edit content on the website at any time. The most heavily trafficked website with historical information is *Wikipedia*, http://en.wikipedia.org, providing background information on close to two million English-language topics (Fig. 7). It is commonly used for historical background research by students, either with or without approval from their teachers. But it is important to remember that each entry in *Wikipedia* is the collective work of multiple authors. You can see the screen name or IP address of the various authors and editors for a given entry by looking at the history tab, a list of all versions of the entry and the changes made (Fig. 8). You may or may not be able to verify the identity or credentials of a given author with this information, however, making it difficult to validate the authority of the entry. How do you know if an author is sharing knowledge, repeating rumors, or purposely posting incorrect information?

Critics reject *Wikipedia* outright as inaccurate because its entries, unlike those in traditional encyclopedias, are the work of non-experts. Supporters argue that *Wikipedia* produces a collective wisdom that is, for the most part, accurate, and that having multiple authors increases the likelihood that someone will catch errors. Both sides raise valid points. Comparisons of entries in *Wikipedia* to those in more traditional encyclopedias like the *Encyclopedia Brittanica* do turn up errors, but the errors appear in both the traditional print encyclopedias and *Wikipedia*. *Wikipedia* entries on popular topics — such as Charles Darwin or the Monroe Doctrine, for instance — are often just as accurate as those in conventional encyclopedias.[6]

---

[5]*Merlot Project* (Multimedia Educational Resource for Learning and Online Teaching), http://www.merlot.org; Internet Scout Project, University of Wisconsin-Madison, *Scout Report*, http://scout.wisc.edu; CHNM and ASHP, *History Matters*, http://historymatters.gmu.edu/browse/wwwhistory/ (all accessed December 18, 2007).

[6]Roy Rosenzweig, "Can History Be Open Source? Wikipedia and the Future of the Past," reprinted from *The Journal of American History* 93, no.1 (June 2006), http://chnm.gmu.edu/resources/essays/d/42 (accessed July 13, 2007).

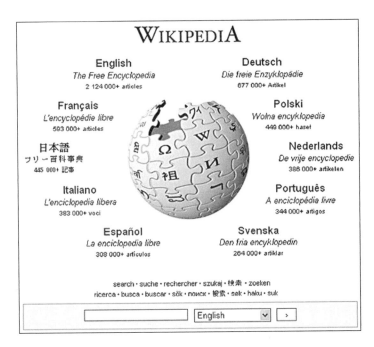

Fig. 7 Screenshot from *Wikipedia*. *(Wikipedia.org)*

To use *Wikipedia* wisely, there are two things to keep in mind. The first is that *Wikipedia* is a collectively authored *encyclopedia*. *Wikipedia* does not value original research; indeed, it prohibits it. Encyclopedias are useful for looking up facts, but they contain little or no interpretation of those facts. The second, given the ever-changing nature of *Wikipedia*, is that *when* you visit an entry matters. Five minutes after your visit, the information may be substantially altered and may even earn the *Wikipedia* warning, "The neutrality and factual accuracy of this article are disputed," that is posted on entries for controversial topics. Re-

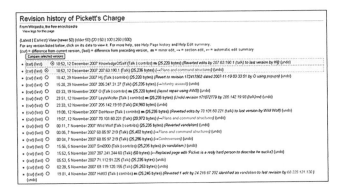

Fig. 8 Screenshot from *Wikipedia*. *(Wikipedia.org)*

cently disputed topics include the "Oklahoma land race" and the "American Mu-toscope and Biograph Company." To cite an entry from *Wikipedia*, include the date and time, available on the "History" tab, to identify which version you used.

A second Web 2.0 development is changing the way we do historical research online. Social networking databases such as the photo-sharing website *Flickr.com* or the video-sharing website *YouTube.com* include new historical content every day. Users of these websites with an interest in the past post historical images and films, such as World War II newsreels or photographs of memorial sites such as monuments or battlegrounds. One significant downside to using this kind of historical material is that it rarely includes any source information, making it difficult or impossible to locate originals or verify origin. On the other hand, these websites often contain material not commonly available. For instance, if you wanted to compare political graffiti across societies or over time, *Flickr.com* might be an excellent resource. Users around the world have made available more than 80,000 photographs of graffiti, including political and historical graf-fiti, that otherwise would be inaccessible without extensive travel, and are un-likely to be included in a traditional online archive (Fig. 9).

Most Web 2.0 sites allow users to interact with content and with each other by editing material directly (as in the case of *Wikipedia*) or by commenting on what they see, read, or watch. The commentary is unlikely to relate to your research, but on occasion, comments can help you make sense of an image or film clip or provide a personal experience connected with it. You may also find visitors to the website who share your interest or have expertise that could help you answer

Fig. 9 Political graffiti from *Flickr.com*. *("America Is Not the World," courtesy of Spencer Eakin.)*

a question. As with the sources themselves, though, proceed with caution and verify authenticity.

History students are taking part in these Web 2.0 developments every day and in the process are participating in the creation of historical content in new ways. Some instructors, for example, require their students to create and edit entries in *Wikipedia*, both because it teaches students about the pros and cons of this online encyclopedia and because it teaches them about the creation of historical information in a public forum. Other students create and edit *Wikipedia* entries on their own because they have an interest in the subject matter. In this way they are taking part in the creation of our common fund of historical knowledge.

Working with Online Primary and Secondary Sources

What is a primary source? What is a secondary source? Knowing the difference between the two categories of materials about the past is important. While both are valuable and useful, they provide different kinds of information and therefore are used, and useful, in different ways (see table below).

Primary Sources and Secondary Sources

Primary Source	Secondary Source
A photograph of Native American dancers in ceremonial dress taken in Alaska in 1895	Analysis of the photograph or the photographers in a history journal
A travel journal documenting eyewitness accounts of North American exploration	A book written by a leading historian in the twenty-first century about seventeenth-century travel writing
An official document such as the Peace Treaty of Versailles	A podcast of a college lecture about the end of World War I
A 1946 newspaper advertisement promising eight daily flights to Memphis, Tennessee	A website on the rise of advertising in the twentieth century or on transportation after World War II
A Work Projects Administration poster on getting tested for syphilis	A scholarly essay about public health in the 1930s
An audio recording of a New Mexican wedding song	Introductory material on a website about music sung by Spanish-speaking residents in New Mexico
An 1880s Sanborn insurance map of Salt Lake City, Utah	A scholarly review of websites presenting Sanborn maps
Data from the first U.S. Census	A study of how data categories have changed since the 1790 census
A child's toy from 1900	A textbook discussion of daily life and play in the United States

Primary sources are materials directly related to the past by time or participation—things created in the past by people living at the time. Historians build their analyses of people, places, and events from these pieces of the past. The category "primary source" includes photographs, prints, paintings, government documents, advertisements, religious symbols, musical recordings, speeches by politicians, films, letters (by ordinary as well as by famous people), newspaper articles, sermons, and material culture such as pottery, furniture, or tools. Primary sources provide the opportunity to engage directly with the past, to try to sort out what happened and why. Working with historical primary sources, however, is not easy. Evidence from the past represents individual experiences as well as social exchanges, and its meaning is rarely obvious at first glance.

Secondary sources are writings by historians and others who generally use primary sources to interpret the past. They provide analysis, interpretation, and summary, placing questions and evidence in a historical context and explaining their significance. Secondary sources invariably reflect the author's point of view as the author shapes historical material, including primary and relevant secondary sources, into an interpretation of the past.

Primary sources are records of the past, the building blocks of history. They require you to be the historian, to investigate the past, interpret materials, and make sense out of the historical record. Primary sources are often incomplete, but they are invaluable because they offer an exciting opportunity to engage directly with the thoughts, ideas, and materials from a particular time period. They illustrate how complex the past can be, challenging you to grapple with uncertainties and to create your own historical arguments. They allow you to develop a convincing argument on historical questions such as whether or not the United States should have dropped an atomic bomb on Japan. Historians seek to do more than just express their opinions on such questions. They use documents, such as military records, newspaper articles, or diaries by Truman, his advisers, and Japanese leaders, some of which can be found at the *Truman Presidential Museum and Library* website [229] to build arguments about the past rooted in historical research.

The following example illustrates the differences between primary and secondary sources. Scholars who study the rise of consumer culture in the twentieth century have disagreed about the cause and effect relationship between advertising and consumer demand. Have advertisers shaped the desires and purchasing habits of consumers? Or have consumers controlled the market while advertisers struggled to follow popular trends?

Michael Schudson, a communications professor who specializes in American media and advertising, argues that advertising does not coerce consumers into buying products. He writes in his book entitled *Advertising, The Uneasy Persuasion* that "Advertising is much less powerful than advertisers and critics of advertising claim, and advertising agencies are stabbing in the dark much more than they are practicing precision microsurgery on the public consciousness."[7]

[7]Michael Schudson, *Advertising, The Uneasy Persuasion: Its Dubious Impact on American Society* (New York: Basic Books, 1996), xiii.

In contrast, Susan Strasser, a history professor who writes about American consumer culture, opens her book *Satisfaction Guaranteed*, on the creation of an American mass market, with the story of Crisco, a new product introduced by Procter and Gamble in 1912. To exert greater influence in the cottonseed oil market, Procter and Gamble "attempted to design consumer demand to meet the needs of production and company growth." They successfully "made Crisco in order to sell it." Strasser argues that the company did not respond to consumer need or demand; they invented a product and through a host of new marketing strategies—grocery promotions, direct mail, free recipe books, recipe contests, and free samples—created a market.[8]

The authors of these two historical books, both secondary sources, present consumer culture and the role of advertising in American life in different ways. They provide examples based on primary sources and develop their analyses to support larger arguments about historical change and cause and effect, but they reach different conclusions. In the following quote from a U.S. history textbook (a different kind of secondary source), a description of the rising twentieth-century consumer culture provides a much broader overview and credits both advertising and consumers as active forces.

> Mass production of a broad range of new products—automobiles, radios, refrigerators, electric irons, washing machines—produced a consumer goods revolution. In this new era of abundance, more people than ever conceived of the American dream in terms of the things they could acquire. . . . The advertising industry linked the possession of material goods to the fulfillment of every spiritual and emotional need. Americans increasingly defined their social status, and indeed their personal worth, in terms of material possessions.[9]

The textbook avoids controversy, stating both that the advertising industry "linked" possessions with needs while consumers "defined their social status" through consumer goods.

A primary source, such as an advertisement, in contrast, offers evidence about the past that you can use to build your argument. Although one primary source alone is not enough to help you answer larger questions about the relationship between consumer demand and market pressure, looking at a range of advertisements can be an excellent way to begin researching this question. Take, for example, this 1923 advertisement for Listerine mouthwash from *Good Housekeeping* magazine (Fig. 10). The text reads, "What secret is your mirror holding back? She was a beautiful girl and talented, too. . . . Yet in the one pursuit that stands foremost in the mind of every girl and woman—marriage—she was a failure."

This advertisement shows how advertisers attempted to influence consumption and exemplifies several common marketing strategies, such as relying on

[8]Susan Strasser, *Satisfaction Guaranteed: The Making of the American Mass Market* (Washington: Smithsonian Institution Press, 1989), 3–28.

[9]James L. Roark et al., *The American Promise*, 3rd ed. (Boston: Bedford/St. Martin's, 2005), 836–38.

Fig. 10 Advertisement, Listerine, 1923.
(Listerine® is a registered trademark of Johnson & Johnson. Used with permission.)

guilt and feelings of inadequacy to influence purchases. According to the ad, this young woman's failures reflected her poor consumer choices (not using Listerine), which the advertisement directly connects to lack of hygiene. Only the use of Listerine, in this scenario, would ensure proper hygiene and, by further extension, social success. The advertisement also highlights the cultural norm that success for women equaled marriage; the advertisement connects being single with failure and further decrees that this is the "fault" of the young woman. Depending on your research question, the next step might be to examine Listerine ads in other publications or from the following year or to compare them with advertisements for other products in the same magazine.[10]

[10]*Good Housekeeping* (July 1923), 175.

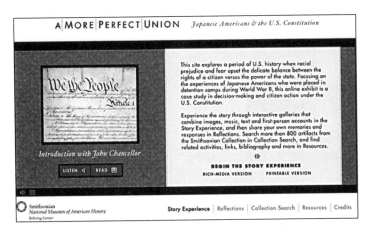

Fig. 11 Screenshot from *A More Perfect Union: Japanese Americans and the U.S. Constitution. (Military History, Smithsonian Institution.)*

The Internet offers a wealth of both primary and secondary sources for understanding the past. The most important thing to keep in mind when using these resources is which kind of source you are examining. Many websites offer either primary materials or secondary interpretations; other websites offer both. For example, the more than 150 websites in the Library of Congress's *American Memory Project* [4] are online archives of primary sources. They include limited contextual material, such as background or interpretive essays, because their central purpose is to offer free access to more than eight million primary sources that can help scholars and students engage with the past and develop their own historical interpretations.

By contrast, online exhibits organized by history teachers, museums, or historical societies often put more emphasis on secondary analysis; they have a particular story to tell and they organize relevant primary sources to tell it. For example, the Smithsonian Institution National Museum of American History website *A More Perfect Union* (Fig. 11) provides an overall narrative of the forced internment of 120,000 Japanese Americans living on the West Coast during World War II. Yet unlike most books on the internment, the exhibit also presents primary sources, including music, personal accounts, artifacts, and images. This website provides a secondary narrative as well as primary sources.[11]

As with textbooks and history books, websites presenting secondary sources, such as explanatory essays or guides, have a point of view. They select certain sources or evidence to address a theme or argue a point. When the point of view is not strongly expressed or reflects widely held views, this bias may not be obvious. Another Smithsonian website, *George Washington: A National Treasure*, presents the first president favorably—a view that most Americans share. But

---

[11]National Museum of American History, "A More Perfect Union," http://americanhistory.si .edu/perfectunion/experience (accessed December 18, 2007).

one reviewer of the website writes that it views Washington in an uncritical manner that is more befitting a monarch than a president.[12]

In other cases, the interpretation presented on a website is more controversial, such as *The Alger Hiss Story: Search for the Truth*, created by author and journalist Jeff Kisseloff. In the 1930s, Whittaker Chambers, a former Communist, accused Alger Hiss, a former State Department official, of providing the Soviet Union with secret documents. Hiss was convicted of perjury and sentenced to five years in prison in a highly publicized case that fueled McCarthyism and spread fear of communism. Hiss's guilt is still debated by historians today. Kisseloff, however, clearly states his belief in Hiss's innocence as well as his goal of creating the website to present the "full facts" of Hiss's life. The secondary source material, in the form of essays, provides layers of analysis supplemented by brief trial excerpts, newspaper clippings, and news footage. This website offers an interesting introduction to the case, but not all historians share Kisseloff's viewpoint and additional research would be required to analyze Alger Hiss in historical perspective.[13]

Some websites present highly controversial viewpoints that are shared by few, if any, serious historians. For example, one can find websites created by those who deny that the Holocaust occurred — a position that no credible historian would embrace. The websites listed in this volume provide a reliable starting point for locating history on the Web.

In most cases, the distinction between primary and secondary sources is clear. In some situations, though, the lines are blurred. A textbook is generally considered a secondary source. In the twenty-first century, however, we might use a textbook from 1960 as a primary source to research what students learned about the Cold War or to what degree history textbooks discussed women's roles in historic events in past decades. Oral history presents another complicated case. Oral histories are usually collected years and even decades after the events being discussed. They are a history of the past and a record of how that past has been remembered as well as a document on how the subject reflects on that past. *Born in Slavery: Slave Narratives from the Federal Writers' Project, 1936–1938* [99], for example, presents oral histories with former slaves collected in the 1930s. The individuals interviewed were between one and fifty years old when slavery ended in 1865; most were more than eighty years old at the time of the interviews. It is important to keep the collection process, elapsed time, and role of memory in mind while analyzing these valuable resources.

When working with primary and secondary sources, it is important to understand that history is not a simple, fixed narrative. Historians debate, discuss, and even disagree about the meaning of various sources and interpretations of the

[12]Smithsonian National Portrait Gallery, "George Washington, A National Treasure," http:// www.georgewashington.si.edu/portrait (accessed December 18, 2007); David Steinberg, "Website Review: George Washington: A National Treasure," *History Matters*, http://historymatters.gmu.edu/ d/6500/ (accessed December 18, 2007).

[13]Jeff Kisseloff, "The Alger Hiss Story: Search for the Truth," http://homepages.nyu.edu/~th15 (accessed December 18, 2007).

past. Many factors shape historical events and historians also look at how things might have happened given different circumstances or when seen through another pair of eyes. For example, our understanding of history changes when we look at the experiences of political leaders versus the daily lives of those who were not known nationally or internationally. Looking at multiple perspectives can provide a more complex understanding of the past. In addition, learning to understand the past, to connect it to a larger story, is key. Equally important is the skill of investigating the past carefully and with an open mind, allowing yourself to see things that may not fit with the larger narrative you have learned.

Here are several important steps historians take when analyzing a primary source:

Sourcing: Start by asking who created the source and what you know about that person or group of people. When and where did it appear? What happened to it after its first appearance? What can we learn about an author's motives, intentions, or point of view? Is the creator in a position to be a good reporter? Why or why not? How did the source survive? Why is it available in the twenty-first century?

Close Reading: Carefully read the source. For a written document, consider the kind of source, tone, and word choice. Pay attention to parts of speech — what kinds of nouns or adjectives are used? Does this remain consistent throughout the document or does it change? How formal or informal is the language? Is the account believable? Is it internally consistent or are there contradictions? For an image, look at each section separately and then look at the whole. Listen to a song or watch a video multiple times. What does the source say or look like or sound like? What might it mean? What does each section mean? How do the sections work together? What questions come up as you carefully analyze the source itself?

Contextualization: Consider the larger historical picture and situate the source within a framework of events and perspectives, paying close attention to *when* they happened and *where* they took place. When was the source created? What else was happening at this time that may have influenced the creator? Where was this source created? How might location have influenced its creation? How might an intended or unintended audience have shaped the source?

Corroboration: Whenever possible, check important details against each other. Evaluate multiple sources in relationship to one another, and look for similarities as well as contradictions. Look at key content and stylistic differences. Where do the sources agree with one another? Where do they disagree? What viewpoint does each source reflect? Which sources seem more reliable or trustworthy? Why?

As you can see, analyzing primary sources requires careful attention to details, language, and historical context. Reading a letter from the eighteenth century is very different from reading a nineteenth-century diary or a twenty-first-century cell phone text message. Analyzing early films requires different skills than interpreting a map. Using new kinds of primary sources to understand the past can be challenging. The website *History Matters* [24] contains a number of guides to "making sense" of different kinds of evidence. In these guides, such as *Making Sense of Maps* or *Making Sense of Films*, and a series of interviews, such as *Analyzing Blues Songs* or *Analyzing Abolitionist Speeches*, scholars suggest questions to ask when working with various kinds of primary sources, from political cartoons to quantitative data.[14]

According to oral historian and scholar Linda Shopes, for example, asking questions such as "Who is talking?" and "Who is the interviewer?" is crucial when reading an oral history interview. The answers provide insight into the circumstances that created the interview as well as the recorded words. Interviewers shape the dynamic of an interview, asking certain questions and responding differently to various kinds of information. The individual being interviewed assesses the interviewer, deciding what he or she can say and what is best left unsaid. For example, a grandparent being interviewed by a grandchild for a family history project may suppress unpleasant memories to protect the child or preserve family myths.[15]

When studying American popular song, historian Ronald G. Walters and musicologist John Spitzer write that there are important issues to investigate in addition to asking who wrote and performed a song. What did the song mean when it was created? Did it mean different things to different audiences? What does it mean now? What can songs tell us about people and society? Musicians and their audiences are social actors. While they reflect the world around them, they also interpret and change it. For every anti–Vietnam War song such as the "I-Feel-Like-I'm-Fixin'-To-Die Rag" (1967), there were pro-war (or anti–anti-war) songs such as the "Ballad of the Green Berets" (1966). In cases such as these, songs are most valuable for telling us what concerned people, how they interpreted various issues, and how they expressed hopes, ideals, and emotions.[16]

An early nineteenth-century inventory of a house and a documentary photograph that came to symbolize the Great Depression in the 1930s demonstrate what can be learned by asking specific questions about resources. In an interview available on the website *History Matters*, historian and museum curator Barbara Clark Smith analyzes an inventory that lists the belongings, including slaves, of a man named Thomas Springer. After Springer's death in 1804, the court in New Castle County, Delaware, appointed appraisers to assess and record the value of his belongings (Fig. 12). Smith shows how the document offers valuable information about the daily life, values, and household goods in this time period, offering insight into the life of someone who was not famous and left few historical artifacts. What did this man own? What can his possessions tell us

[14]*Making Sense of Evidence* guides (*Making Sense of Documents*) and interviews (*Scholars in Action*), http://historymatters.gmu.edu/browse/makesense.

[15]See Linda Shopes, *Making Sense of Oral History*, http://historymatters.gmu.edu/mse/oral.

[16]See Ronald G. Walters and John Spitzer, *Making Sense of American Popular Song*, http://history matters.gmu.edu/mse/songs.

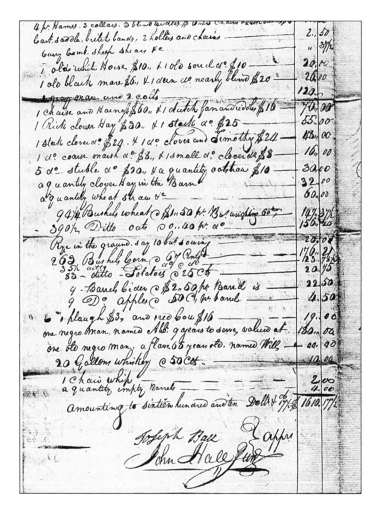

Fig. 12 An inventory of the belongings of Thomas Springer after his death in 1804. The value of Springer's possessions informs research into the economic and cultural conditions of his time. Of particular interest are "one negro man, named Ace[?]: 9 years to serve, valued at 180.00" and "one old negro man, a slave 66 years old, named Will . . . 00.00." What can we learn from this information? *(Courtesy of Delaware Public Archives.)*

about his life? What can we learn about the lives of others in his household, such as his wife and two African American men?[17]

This inventory begins with the clothing of the deceased, including coats, shirts, trousers, and boots. The dollar amount assigned to various items provides a sense of what they might have cost. Clothing was valuable, worth $30 in 1804. This was more valuable than the "feather Bed, Bedding and Bedstead"

[17]See Barbara Clark Smith, *Analyzing an 1804 Inventory,* **http://historymatters.gmu.edu/mse/ sia/inventory.htm.**

valued at $26. The inventory also reveals some family behavior and patterns. The teacups and tea table suggest participation in the ceremony of tea. "Two spinning wheels" hints at the work done by women in the Springer household.

Perhaps more surprising is that people are listed among the artifacts, including two "negro" men. This reveals several important things about the period and the status of slaves. In some respects, this was common practice—these men are listed as possessions alongside clocks and trousers. But it is also interesting to note that only one is listed as a slave. In Delaware in 1804, slavery was ending, primarily because it was not as profitable in the North as it was in the South. The "negro man named Ace" had "nine years to serve." This suggests that Ace may have negotiated his freedom for a certain number of years of service, an indenture to the Springers, which some African Americans did after the American Revolution. At the end of the set period, Ace would have received his freedom and possibly a small amount of money. "Will," however, is described as a slave and no monetary value is placed on him, probably because of his age.

With strategies for analyzing the inventory, we can learn about daily life, economics, social relationships, and work from this one document. The inventory can be even more valuable when compared with similar lists from Springer's town or county and with those from neighboring areas. Examining inventories over a period of ten years would reveal what different people owned, which items were typical, and which things were extraordinary. With a large enough pool of inventories, you could start to count the items involved and utilize quantitative analysis to study trends.

Reading an inventory may seem relatively straightforward, but there are often vast amounts of information hiding beneath the surface. It can also appear easy to look at a photograph and mistakenly think of it as a reproduction of reality, a historical mirror. Historian James Curtis discusses how visual evidence requires different tools of analysis in his guide, *Making Sense of Documentary Photography*. Scholars ask who wrote a letter or autobiography and why, but it is equally important to ask who took a photograph. Why was it taken? Who sponsored it? What was the photographer's goal or intent in taking the image? How was the photograph taken and how was it presented to the public? There are important stories hidden within images that can teach us many things about the past.[18]

Documentary photography emerged in the second half of the nineteenth century and was initially considered journalism rather than art. Documentary photographers were seen as event recorders and they often encouraged this misconception, presenting themselves as fact gatherers and denying political or social motives. It is impossible, though, even with a goal of recording events, to avoid shaping a picture. Photographers make many decisions as they create an image regarding subject, angle, framing, what to include, and equally important, what to exclude. Printing, selecting, editing, and presentation shape the final

---

[18]See James Curtis, *Making Sense of Documentary Photography,* **http://historymatters.gmu .edu/mse/Photos**.

Fig. 13 *Rebel Sharpshooter in Devil's Den*, photograph. *(Library of Congress, Prints & Photographs Division, reproduction number LC-B8171-7942 DLC.)*

product and all of these decisions are influenced by the photographer's goals, as well as mechanical limitations.

During the Civil War, as Curtis writes, bulky equipment and long exposure times meant that photographers could not capture combatants in action. Instead, they took pictures of battlefield remains, sometimes rearranging scenes for dramatic effect. After the bloody battle of Gettysburg in 1863, photographer Alexander Gardner had a dead soldier moved across a field and placed in a rocky corner. The resulting photograph, *Rebel Sharpshooter in Devil's Den*, remains a powerful image of the Civil War despite knowledge of the photographer's intervention (Fig. 13).[19]

Manipulation of subjects remains an important tool for documentary photographers. This becomes apparent when looking at companion photographs. Documentary photographers often take a series of pictures to ensure backup images. The process also provides the opportunity to later select an image that best relates their sense of the scene or reflects the meaning they want to present. Photographers working for the Farm Security Administration (FSA) during the Great Depression were required to submit all of their negatives from an assignment, creating an amazing record of companion photographs that detail the steps involved in obtaining a desired image. A collection of these photographs is

[19]American Memory Project, Library of Congress, *Rebel Sharpshooter in Devil's Den* (or *The Home of a Rebel Sharpshooter, Gettysburg*), http://memory.loc.gov/ammem/cwphtml/cwphome.html (accessed October 15, 2003).

Fig. 14 Dorothea Lange's photo series; *Migrant Mother*, bottom right. *(Library of Congress, Prints & Photographs Division, 1936.)*

available at the Library of Congress website *America from the Great Depression to World War II: Photographs from the FSA-OWI, 1935–1945* [187].[20]

One of the most enduring images of the Depression, known as *Migrant Mother*, depicts a woman and her children in a California migrant labor camp (Fig. 14). This is the last in a series of six photographs that FSA photographer Dorothea Lange took on a rainy afternoon in March 1936. The composition of this image, however, was not accidental. Lange crafted the photograph carefully, changing perspective and camera angles, excluding details and people, and rearranging poses.

These images demonstrate Lange's control of the scene and the action of her subjects. In her initial frame, Lange showed thirty-four-year-old Florence Thompson and four of her children. In the second frame, the oldest of the four is outside the tent. Thompson had seven children, but Lange knew this would not elicit sympathy from her middle-class audience and concentrated on the youngest ones. The trunk and empty pie tin in the foreground of the fifth photograph attest to the family's itinerancy and struggle for survival, but they do not appear in the final frame. For the sixth photograph, Lange posed the two young girls with their heads resting on their mother's shoulders. She turned their faces away from the camera and brought Thompson's right hand to her face, a strategy for framing the face and drawing attention to the subject's feelings. This final picture was as Lange had envisioned and quickly became a symbol for the suffering occasioned by the Great Depression coupled with the strength of human dignity. The companion images, though, show that this was not a simple document or a reflection of reality. The image and its message were shaped by Lange, her purpose, her sponsor, and her audience.[21]

Learning various strategies to analyze historical evidence creates new opportunities and introduces new questions. When you think carefully about the kinds of materials you are using and what they tell you that other resources cannot, your research question will become more refined and you may be led to unexpected conclusions. Start by asking general questions, move to specific questions relevant for that source, and then explore how the primary source fits into a larger context.

Search Tips and Further Resources

Using Search Engines Effectively

Browsing is very helpful when you are starting a project and do not have a specific resource or topic in mind. A well-designed website allows you to wander around large thematic or chronological sections, to see connections and groupings. When you do know what you want, however, a keyword search is sometimes

[20]American Memory Project, Library of Congress, *America from the Great Depression to World War II: Photographs from the FSA–OWI, 1935–1945*, http://memory.loc.gov/ammem/fsowhome.html.

[21]For more on the *Migrant Mother* photograph, see *What Can Companion Images Tell Us* at http://historymatters.gmu.edu/mse/photos/question4.html.

the best path. *Google*, the most commonly used search engine, can be a powerful tool, especially once you understand how it works and how to use it wisely.

The first wave of search engines, such as *AltaVista*, *HotBot*, and *Excite*, were not very successful at discriminating between high-quality and low-quality websites. A poorly written website that mentioned the Holocaust fifty times might be mechanically ranked more "relevant" than an authoritative website from the *U.S. Holocaust Memorial Museum* [206] that mentioned the word only a dozen times on its homepage. In the late 1990s, *Google* revolutionized the way search engines work, presenting a smarter search engine.

Google looks at the presence of keywords in the title and URL rather than searching meta tags, the hidden tags written by a website author to describe the contents of a webpage. The more significant development, however, builds on a unique element of the Web itself—the ability to link to other websites. *Google* founders Larry Page and Sergey Brin found a way to use the popularity of certain websites to promote their rankings. A website on the Holocaust with twenty links to it from other websites was probably better than a site with one or two links to it. If in turn some of those other websites were "authoritative" (*i.e.,* they also had lots of links to them), so much the better for the first website's ranking. In short, *Google* found a way to measure reputation on the Web through a recursive analysis of the interconnectedness of the medium itself.[22]

Here are some useful tips for using a search engine:

Use Quotation Marks   Using quotation marks makes your search more specific by identifying multiple search terms as a specific phrase. If you enter the words *U.S. history* without quotes, *Google* returns more than 130 million results. If you put the search term in quotes ("U.S. history") you narrow it to six million. Entering the specific topic, time period, or region you are interested in exploring, such as "U.S. history" "scopes trial," will narrow it still further.

Use Advanced Search   The easiest way to expedite your search and quickly move from millions of returns to hundreds or even dozens, is to use the *Advanced Search* feature. You can click on "Advanced Search" from *Google*'s main search page or go directly to **http://www.google.com/advanced_search**. This allows you to narrow your search to specific languages, include or exclude words or phrases, restrict domain names, or define the location of occurrences (*e.g.,* the phrase occurs anywhere on the page, only in the title, or only in the text of a webpage).

Enter Multiple Terms   If you are interested in the role played by American troops in the Boxer Rebellion, "boxer rebellion American troops" will help you avoid websites on the boxer Muhammad Ali. The first website returned by the *Google* search engine in this search is the *Wikipedia* page on the Boxer Rebellion. The second website is from the National Archives and offers an article

---

[22]Daniel J. Cohen and Roy Rosenzweig, "Building an Audience: Mass Marketing, Online and Off," *Digital History: A Guide to Gathering, Preserving, and Presenting the Past on the Web*, University of Pennsylvania Press, **http://chnm.gmu.edu/digitalhistory/audience/2.php** (accessed July 16, 2007).

(secondary source) on the involvement of American troops in the rebellion. The third choice is from the Public Broadcasting Service (PBS), and includes the transcript of an interview with noted American diplomatic historian Walter LaFeber. The fourth is from *About.com*, which simply republishes the content from *Wikipedia*. It is not until you get to the ninth choice in the *Google* search that you finally have access to primary sources, in this case drawn from a U.S. Navy collection.

Tell Google *Where to Find It*   If you know that you saw a handwritten Jewish calendar from 1844 on the website *Jews in America: Our Story* [31], but do not remember exactly where on the website you found it, you can type your keyword and the URL "calendar 1844 site: www.jewsinamerica.org" into a *Google* search. This will take you to a searchable image gallery list where you can quickly find the calendar. If you remember that the title of a website you visited included the words "historic," "building," and "survey" you can type "intitle:historic building survey" to quickly find *Built in America: Historic American Buildings Survey and Historic American Engineering Record* [10].

Other such operators include

intext:	*inurl:*
allintext:	*author:*
allintitle:	*location:*

Use the +, –, |, and ~ Signs   It is also possible to limit the results of a *Google* search by using special characters. If you are interested in listening directly to the words of Samuel Gompers, you might search for "Samuel Gompers" + "audio." The first hit is the American Memory Project website *American Leaders Speak: Recordings from World War I and the 1920 Election* [143]. The minus sign (–) means *not* and the solid vertical line (|) substitutes for *or*. If you are searching for information on the John Scopes trial, you might try "John Scopes | monkey + trial" because the case was also called the "Monkey" trial. Or, if you wanted search results that *excluded Wikipedia*, you would use "John Scopes | monkey – wikipedia" to access more carefully selected search results. If you are not sure about different names for the same thing, try using the synonym search. Using the tilde (~) symbol in your search returns the term you are looking for *and* any synonyms of that term.

Translate a Text   Although a rough translator at best, *Google* can give you the "gist" of an article or website in a number of languages, including Arabic, Chinese, French, German, Italian, Japanese, Korean, Russian, Portuguese, and Spanish. See **http://www.google.com/language_tools** for this feature. Beware, however, that free, online translations are mechanically generated and are often imperfect.

Other Searches   You can find a current street or satellite map by typing an address into *Google* or using *Google Maps* at **http://maps.google.com**. You can also find out what a word means by asking *Google*. For example, enter "define:portmanteau" to find the two possible meanings of *portmanteau*. You can also convert measurements or make a calculation with *Google*. Type "9000/4" and *Google* will return the answer "2250." Type "35 degrees Celsius in Fahrenheit" and you will receive "95 degrees Fahrenheit."

Other Search Engines   When searching for information on current events, you may want to search directly on media websites such as the *New York Times*, http://www.nytimes.com, or the *British Broadcasting Corporation*, http://www.bbc.co.uk. Both offer broad coverage of current events, although access to archived articles is not free. You can also try other search engines such as *Metacrawler*, http://www.metacrawler.com, and *Vivísimo*, http://www.vivisimo.com. Keep a library of "favorites" or "bookmarks" with search engines or websites that you use frequently for research.

A Word About Plagiarism

Printed materials have long provided ready content for plagiarism, but the Internet, and the mixture of skill and naiveté with which many approach it, creates new opportunities and new dangers. Online texts, images, sounds, and videos are easy to copy, paste, and manipulate. While this may make note taking easier, it also makes plagiarism—intentional or unintentional—as easy as clicking on "copy" and "paste." Many students are not aware of the full meaning of plagiarism and its repercussions. School and college policies vary, but students who are caught plagiarizing can encounter a range of consequences, from failing a course to expulsion. Plagiarism does not have to be deliberate to be wrong— unintentional plagiarism is generally subject to the same penalties.[23]

Plagiarism is presenting the words, work, or opinions of someone else as one's own without proper acknowledgment. This includes borrowing the sequence of ideas, the arrangement of material, or the pattern of thought from someone else without proper acknowledgment. If a history paper gives the impression that the writer of the paper is the author of the words, ideas, or conclusions when they are the product of another person's work, the writer of that paper is guilty of plagiarism. This is equally true for published and unpublished materials (such as a paper written by another student) as well as for any material found on the Internet.

Studying other people's ideas through primary and secondary sources is central to conducting historical research. Historians use quotations from primary sources to illustrate their arguments and include quotations from other scholars to place their discussion in a larger context. Both of these uses are acceptable, and indeed desirable, aspects of writing a history paper. The key is to always credit the source of direct quotations, paraphrased information, or ideas, and to use your skills to create your own original ideas and historical analysis.

---

[23]Johns Hopkins University History Department guidelines; Diana Hacker, *The Bedford Handbook for Writers*, 4th ed. (New York: St. Martin's, 1994), 477–79; *Bedford/St. Martin's Workshop on Plagiarism*, bedfordstmartins.com/plagiarism/flyer.

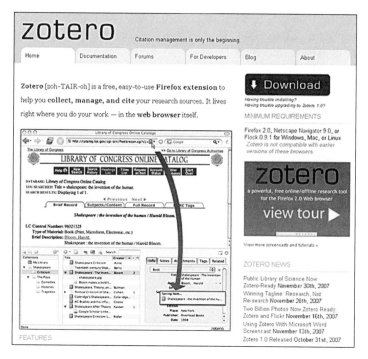

Fig. 15 Screenshot from *Zotero*. *(Center for History and New Media, George Mason University.)*

There are new tools to help you in this process. *Zotero*, **http://www.zotero.org/**, a free extension for the popular open-source web browser *Firefox*, allows you to build, organize, and annotate your own collections while conducting research online (Fig. 15). With the click of a mouse, it collects and saves all available reference information about a website, book, article, or other primary source from major research websites and databases, such as *JSTOR*, *ProQuest*, and *Google Books*, as well as most library catalogs. Once saved into *Zotero*, you can add notes, drag and drop texts and images into multiple collections (folders), search your collections, export citations, and create "reports" or documents summarizing your research. You can also highlight and add notes to stored documents from the Web. Tools such as *Zotero* help you organize your research and reduce the risk of ending up with unidentified sources or notes, a key factor in avoiding plagiarism.[24]

Here are some steps that you can take to avoid plagiarism.

1) Start by taking notes carefully, especially when moving from a website to a word processing document or when typing notes from a book. If you copy and paste, always put the entire text in quotes and include the full citation. If you paraphrase, make sure that you understand the original text and

---

[24]For more information, see Daniel J. Cohen, "Zotero: Social and Semantic Computing for Historical Scholarship," *Perspectives* (May 2007), **http://www.historians.org/Perspectives/issues/2007/0705/0705tec2.cfm** (accessed June 29, 2007).

then put it aside. Write the idea in your own words and be sure to cite the author as the source of the idea, even when it is not a direct quote.

2) When you quote directly from a source to a computer document (including all citation information), change the color of the quote with your word processor to make it stand out from the rest of the text. This will serve as a visual reminder that something is a quote and requires proper citation.

3) Update your list of sources, primary and secondary, as you take notes. Use the guidelines for citing electronic resources listed below.

4) Keep a copy of each source you use, including photocopies of print articles and key passages from books. Print copies of online sources or email them to yourself and store them together in one folder.

5) Save drafts of your work as you research and write papers. When you begin to make revisions, create a new copy and save the original. This creates a record of your work and the development of your thoughts.

6) Finally, learn more about plagiarism, paraphrasing, and college regulations by visiting a writing center or library. Visit the websites listed below for additional definitions, suggestions, and resources.

Additional Online Resources on Research, Plagiarism, and Documenting Sources:

> *Research and Documentation Online*, Diana Hacker
>   http://dianahacker.com/resdoc
> *Writer's Handbook*, University of Wisconsin-Madison, Writing Center
>   http://www.wisc.edu/writing/Handbook
> *Documenting Sources*, George Mason University Writing Center
>   http://writingcenter.gmu.edu/resources/plagiarism.html

Citing Online Sources

Citing sources is key to conducting historical research. It also provides an important record of your research process. Keeping a "running" bibliography of print and online sources, whether you are using a program such as *Zotero* or in a word processing document, helps you assess what sources you are using, the balance of primary and secondary materials, and whether or not you need to seek out new kinds of sources to gain a well-rounded perspective on an issue.

Footnotes for a history assignment may vary slightly from those required in other courses. Here are some guidelines to follow for citing various kinds of electronic sources if you do not receive specific instructions in class. The following guidelines are based on *The Chicago Manual of Style*, fifteenth edition, and are specific for footnotes or endnotes. For bibliography or reference list styles, visit *The Chicago Manual of Style Online* "Citation Quick Guide," http://www .chicagomanualofstyle.org/tools_citationguide.html.[25]

---

[25]University of Chicago Press, "Chicago-Style Citation Quick Guide," *The Chicago Manual of Style Online*, 15th ed. (2006), http://www.chicagomanualofstyle.org/tools_citationguide.html (accessed June 28, 2007).

Website   List the author or organization that is responsible for the website, followed by the title of the subsection in quotation marks (if relevant) and the website title in italics, each separated by a comma. Next, list the URL and the date of access in parentheses.

> University of Connecticut Libraries, *Colonial Connecticut Records, 1636–1776,* http://www.colonialct.uconn.edu/ (accessed December 8, 2007).

> U.S. Department of State, Office of the Historian, "Kennedy Administration," *Foreign Relations of the United States,* http://www.state.gov/r/pa/ho/frus/kennedyjf/ (accessed December 15, 2007).

Source from an Online Database   List the author of the source (if available) followed by the name of the source in quotation marks, name of the database in italics, URL, and date accessed.

> John Quincy Adams, "Liberty Incomplete," 1843, *Samuel J. May Anti-Slavery Collection,* http://dlxs.library.cornell.edu/cgi/t/text/pageviewer-idx?c=mayantislavery;idno=07838115;view=image;seq=1 (accessed November 30, 2007).

Book Published Electronically   List the author(s) of the book, followed by the title, publisher, URL, and date accessed.

> Daniel J. Cohen and Roy Rosenzweig, *Digital History: A Guide to Gathering, Preserving, and Presenting the Past on the Web,* University of Pennsylvania Press, http://chnm.gmu.edu/digitalhistory/book.php (accessed June 28, 2007).

Journal Article Published Electronically   List the author(s) of the article, article title in quotation marks, journal title and publication information, publisher, URL, and date accessed.

> Andrea Friedman, "The Strange Career of Annie Lee Moss: Rethinking Race, Gender, and McCarthyism," *The Journal of American History* (September 2007), http://mutex.gmu.edu:2069/journals/jah/94.2/friedman.html (accessed December 16, 2007).

Weblog (Blog) Entry or Comment   List the author of the entry or comment, followed by identifying information on the entry or comment, name of the blog, date posted, URL, and date accessed.

> Mills Kelly, entry on "What's It All About?" *Edwired,* entry posted on June 6, 2007, http://edwired.org/?p=183 (accessed June 28, 2007).

> Jonathan Dresner, "Teacher Logic," comment on "History At Play," Rob MacDougall, *CLIOPATRIA: A Group Blog,* comment posted on June 27, 2007, http://hnn.us/blogs/entries/40294.html (accessed June 29, 2007).

Email Message   List the author of the email, identify it as an email message, include the subject header when possible, and add the date on which it was sent. If the email is personal, note that but do not include the author's email address. Ask permission from the author before citing a personal email message.

Lynn Temple, "Re: Question about the Bedford flag," email message, March 26, 2007.

Listserv Message   The format is similar to an email message, but you should include the email address of the listserv.

Liz Ten Dyke, "South Asians in 19th century USA," listserv message, January 17, 2003, **h-world@h-net.msu.edu**.

Using This Guide

Online resources for learning about U.S. history have opened an exciting world of primary materials and analysis to college students everywhere. To take full advantage of these opportunities, learn to find reliable websites, beginning with those listed in this guide. Then start to think about strategies for critically analyzing the range of online sources you can access, asking questions specific to the kinds of sources you are using.

The collection of 250 websites included in this book is not definitive; rather, it is intended as a useful guide to finding valuable online resources for exploring the American past. The authors of this book reviewed more than 5,000 websites to select this list with the goal of illustrating the strengths of the Internet for learning about the past and the incredible range of resources and perspectives available, from images of the Atlantic slave trade [57] through *Washington Post* news stories leading to Richard Nixon's resignation in *Watergate Revisited* [250]. Many excellent websites were not included, but those we have chosen represent some of the best materials available for use in a U.S. history course.

Most of the websites presented here are available at no cost. Increasingly, however, publishers are creating significant historical databases and charging subscription fees. If colleges and universities subscribe to these databases, the materials become available for student use. Fees range widely and can be quite high, but some of these websites offer large quantities of materials otherwise unavailable, such as historical newspapers and periodicals. *ProQuest Information and Learning* [46] allows access to the *New York Times* (1851–2001), the *Washington Post* (1877–1988), the *Wall Street Journal* (1889–1986), and the *Christian Science Monitor* (1908–1991) as well as a host of other resources. *Accessible Archives* [83] provides close to 200,000 articles from nineteenth-century newspapers, magazines, and books, including *Godey's Lady's Book* (1830–1880), one of the most popular nineteenth-century publications, and the *Pennsylvania Gazette* (1728–1800). *HarpWeek* [125] offers some resources at no cost as well as subscription-based access to full-text images and transcriptions from *Harper's Weekly* (1857–1912). Given the size and scope of these resources, some subscription websites are included in this guide. Their status is clearly identified in the description and the symbol for subscription websites 💰 is included. Ask your librarian if your school subscribes to these resources, and how you can access them. If you do not currently have access, read the information available on the website. Some offer trial subscriptions or low cost access for individual students.

Additional symbols note the kinds of resources available on each website. ▤ signifies that there are significant textual primary sources, such as books, documents, letters, or diaries. ▨ includes photographs, paintings, or drawings. ◀)) means that audio files, usually music, speeches, or oral history interviews, are available. ▥ means that the website offers film or video clips, ranging from early film footage to contemporary commercials and interviews. ▥ indicates quantitative resources, such as census or price data. ⊕ identifies the presence of cartographic resources.

The first section of this list, "General Websites for U.S. History Research," introduces resources that span broad periods of time. Some of these provide a broad range of resources, such as the National Archives and Record Administration database, *Archival Research Catalog (ARC)* [7] or *Hypertext on American History from the Colonial Period until Modern Times* [26], created by a history professor in the Netherlands. Others deal with a specific topic or kind of resource across centuries, such as *Women and Social Movements in the United States, 1600–2000* [55] created by history professors Thomas Dublin and Kathryn Kish Sklar or *American Time Capsule: Three Centuries of Broadsides and Printed Ephemera* [6] from the Library of Congress's American Memory Project collection.

The subsequent sections focus on broad time periods covered in U.S. history survey courses.

Three Worlds Meet and Colonization, Beginnings to 1763

Revolution and the New Nation, 1754–1820s

Expansion and Reform, 1801–1861

Civil War and Reconstruction, 1850–1877

Development of the Industrial United States, 1870–1900

Emergence of Modern America, 1890–1930

Great Depression and World War II, 1929–1945

Postwar United States, 1945 to the Early 1970s

Contemporary United States, 1968 to Present

Finally, the index is a valuable starting point if you are looking for resources on a general topic (e.g., "African Americans," "International Relations," or "Women"), specific events or individuals (e.g., "Mark Twain" or "World War I"), or for a particular kind of primary source (e.g., "Advertising," "Music," or "Speeches"). The glossary provides definitions of common Internet terms.

The Internet can help you track down answers to historical questions or explore unique primary sources to challenge traditional explanations in American history. Use it wisely and it can be a valuable tool for learning about the past.

—Kelly Schrum

Key to the Icons

📄 This website contains written primary sources, such as literary works, official documents, letters, or diaries.

🖼 This website contains images, such as photographs, paintings, drawings, and artifacts.

🔊 This website contains audio files, such as music, speeches, or oral history interviews.

🎬 This website contains film or video clips.

📊 This website contains quantitative resources, such as census or price data.

🌐 This website contains maps and other cartographic resources.

💰 This website charges a fee.

2

A Selection of Top U.S. History Websites

GENERAL WEBSITES FOR U.S. HISTORY RESEARCH

1. Africans in America

PBS Online
http://www.pbs.org/wgbh/aia/

Created as a companion to the PBS series of the same name, this well produced website traces the history of Africans in America through Reconstruction in four chronological parts. The website provides 245 documents, images, and maps linked to a narrative essay. "The Terrible Transformation" (1450–1750) deals with the beginning of the slave trade and slavery's growth. "Revolution" (1750–1805) discusses the justifications for slavery in the new nation. "Brotherly Love" (1791–1831) traces the development of the abolition movement. "Judgment Day" (1831–1865) describes debates over slavery, the strengthening of sectionalism, and the Civil War. In addition to the documents, images, maps, and essays, the website presents 153 brief descriptions by historians of specific aspects on the history of slavery, abolition, and war in America. The website provides a valuable introduction to the study of African American history through the Civil War.

2. Alexander Street Press

Alexander Street Press
http://alexanderstreet.com/

Offering close to twenty separate databases of digitized materials, this website provides first-hand accounts (diaries, letters, and memoirs) and literary efforts (poetry, drama, and fiction). Twelve databases pertain to American history and culture. "Early Encounters in North America: Peoples, Cultures, and the Environment" documents cultural interactions from 1534 to 1850. "The American Civil War: Letters and Diaries" draws on more than 400 sources and supplies a day-by-day chronology with links to documents. "Black Thought and Culture" furnishes monographs, speeches, essays, articles, and interviews. "North American Immigrant Letters, Diaries, and Oral Histories" covers 1840 to the present. "North American Women's Letters and Diaries: Colonial to 1950" provides full-text letters and diaries written between 1675 and 1950 by more than 1,000 women. Five databases present American literary writings: "Latino Literature," "Black Drama," "Asian American Drama," "North American Women's Drama," and "American Film Scripts Online." In addition, "Oral History Online" provides a reference work with links to texts, audio, and video files. While these databases include previously published documents, many also contain thousands of pages of unpublished material. Along with keyword searching, the databases provide "semantic indexing"—extensive categorical search capabilities.

3. American Journeys

Wisconsin Historical Society and National History Day
http://www.americanjourneys.org

These 181 first-hand accounts of North American and Canadian exploration range from Viking stories such as "The Saga of Eric the Red" from circa 1000 C.E. to journal entries written in the early nineteenth century on a trapping expedition in the southwest. Documents include the "Original Journals of the Lewis and Clark Expedition, 1804–1806." Additional materials include rare books, original manuscripts, and classic travel narratives. Users can view the full archive or browse by expedition, settlement, geographic region, and U.S. state or Canadian province. Each document is individually searchable and accompanied by a short background essay and a reference map. There are also 150 images available, including woodcuts, drawings, paintings, and photographs. "Highlights" follows the collection chronologically and connects moments in American history with eyewitness accounts.

4. American Memory: Historical Collections for the National Digital Library

American Memory Project, Library of Congress
http://lcweb2.loc.gov/amhome.html

This expansive archive of American history and culture features more than nine million items dating from 1490 to the present. Strengths include the early republic, with documents and papers on the Continental Congress, U.S. Congress, early Virginia religious petitions, George Washington, and Thomas Jefferson; the Civil War, including Abraham Lincoln's papers and Mathew Brady photographs; and exploration and settlement of the West. Collections offer papers of inventors, such as Alexander Graham Bell, Emile Berliner, Samuel F. B. Morse, and the Wright Brothers, and composers, such as Leonard Bernstein and Aaron Copland. The website also features New Deal–era documentation projects, such as Farm Security Administration photographs, Federal Writers' Project life histories, the Historic American Buildings Survey, and the Library's own "Man on the Street" interviews following the Pearl Harbor attack. Entertainment history is amply represented with collections on the American Variety Stage, Federal Theatre Project, early cinema, and early sound recordings. African American history, ethnic history, women's history, folk music, sheet music, maps, and photography also are well documented. Digitized images from materials not included in specific *American Memory Project* websites may be searched using the Library's "Prints & Photographs Online Catalog" (**http://lcweb .loc.gov/rr/print/catalog.html**).

5. American President: An Online Reference Resource

Miller Center of Public Affairs, University of Virginia
http://millercenter.org/academic/americanpresident/

Information on all forty-three of the nation's presidents is presented on this website. Each president is featured individually with an in-depth biographical essay, details about the first lady and members of the Cabinet, links to the President's speeches, and discussions with current scholars. The Presidency as an institution is treated thoroughly in the "President at Work" section with essays on general areas of presidential duty: domestic and economic policy, national security, legislative affairs, administration of the government and White House, and presidential politics. Clicking on "Presidential Oral Histories" or "Presidential Recordings" under the "Academic Programs" tab reveals an additional wealth of information. Recordings are available for Presidents Roosevelt, Truman, Eisenhower, Kennedy, Johnson, and Nixon. After tapes were prohibited from the Oval Office following the Watergate scandal, the Miller Center began to conduct oral history projects, producing hours of interviews with Presidents Carter, Reagan, Bush, and Clinton and their staff.

6. American Time Capsule: Three Centuries of Broadsides and Printed Ephemera

American Memory Project, Library of Congress
http://memory.loc.gov/ammem/rbpehtml/

This website furnishes more than 10,000 items of ephemera—"transitory documents created for a specific purpose, and intended to be thrown away." Items come from the United States and London, and date from the seventeenth century to the present, though the majority are from the nineteenth century. Materials include posters, advertisements, leaflets, propaganda, and business cards, and relate to subjects such as the American Revolution, slavery, western migration, the Civil War, the Industrial Revolution, travel, labor, education, health, and woman's suffrage. Users can search by keyword or browse by author, title, genre, or printing location. The website offers a special presentation on popular types of broadsides and ephemera. These resources are valuable for studying popular print, consumer culture, and issues of public concern to ordinary people.

7. Archival Research Catalog (ARC)

National Archives and Records Administration (NARA)
http://www.archives.gov/research/arc/index.html

ARC offers more than 78,000 digital government resources (and continues to expand). Materials include textual records, photographs, maps, architectural drawings, artifacts, sound recordings, and motion pictures dating from the colonial period to the recent past. ARC includes items on presidents, the military, war, immigration, Japanese American internment, slavery, science, prisons, federal programs, the environment, the National Park Service, foreign affairs, civil rights, African Americans, and Native Americans. To begin a search, click on the yellow "search" button near the top left corner of the ARC webpage. The search engine is clearly organized and invites queries on specific historical materials or general themes. To access *only* digitized materials, check the box marked "Descriptions of Archival Materials linked to digital copies."

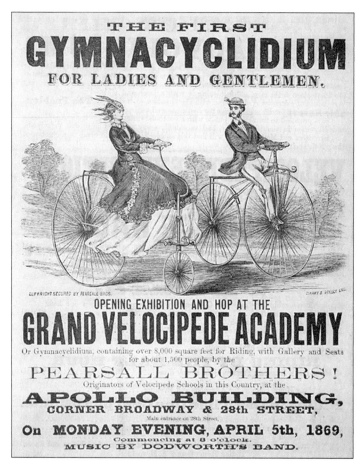

Broadside, 1869, from *American Time Capsule: Three Centuries of Broadsides and Printed Ephemera* [6]. *(Library of Congress, Rare Book and Special Collections Division.)*

8. Avalon Project: Documents in Law, History, and Government

Yale Law School

http://www.yale.edu/lawweb/avalon/avalon.htm

The more than 3,500 full-text documents available on this website address U.S. legal, economic, political, diplomatic, and governmental history. Documents are divided into five time periods—pre-eighteenth, eighteenth, nineteenth, twentieth, and twenty-first centuries—and include treaties, presidential papers and addresses, and colonial charters, as well as state and federal constitutional and legal documents. The materials are categorized into sixty-four document collections as well, such as "American Revolution," "Federalist Papers," "Slavery," "Native Americans," "Confederate States of America," "World War II," "Cold War," "Indochina," "Soviet-

American Diplomacy," and "September 11, 2001." By clicking "What's New," the latest digitized documents become available. Material also can be accessed through an alphabetical list of 350 specific categories. Documents focus on American history, but some materials address European and modern diplomatic history.

9. Battle Lines: Letters from America's Wars

Gilder Lehrman Institute and the Legacy Project
http://www.gilderlehrman.org/collection/battlelines/index_good.html

Both the personal and political sides of Americans engaged in warfare come to life through this annotated collection of more than thirty letters. These letters cover conflicts from the Revolutionary War to the current war in Iraq and are divided thematically into five sections: "Enlisting," "Comforts of Home," "Love," "Combat," and "The End of the War." Letters from well-known military figures, such as Douglas MacArthur and Robert E. Lee, as well as unknown veterans, such as Peter Kiterage, one of the 5,000 African Americans who fought in the Revolutionary War, are included. The thematic organization allows users to chart changes and continuities over 200 years of American history. Audio recordings present readings of the letters and a "magic lens" feature shows typed text over handwritten script.

10. Built in America: Historic American Buildings Survey and Historic American Engineering Record

American Memory Project, Library of Congress, and National Parks Service
http://memory.loc.gov/ammem/collections/habs_haer/

These facsimile images of measured drawings, photographs, and written documentation cover 35,000 significant historic sites dating from the seventeenth to the twentieth centuries. The Historic American Buildings Survey (HABS) started in 1933 as a work relief program and became a permanent part of the National Park Service the following year to document "our architectural heritage of buildings," in the words of project founder Charles E. Peterson. The Historic American Engineering Record (HAER) was established in 1969 to similarly survey engineering works and industrial sites. For each structure, the website provides up to ten drawings, thirty photographs, and fifty pages of HABS text detailing the structure's history, significance, and current physical condition. The collection displays building types and engineering technologies from a farmhouse to a pickle factory, from churches to the Golden Gate Bridge.

11. Campaign Atlases

Major Robert Bateman, U.S. Military Academy
http://www.dean.usma.edu/history/web03/atlases/AtlasesTableOfContents.html

This website is particularly useful for studying cartography and military history. The 400 twentieth-century color maps of military campaigns cover a broad range of conflicts, from American colonial wars to U.S. involvement in Somalia in the early 1990s. Most of the maps represent conflicts in which the United States played a role, such as the "Battle of Bunker Hill" or the "Allied Landing in Normandy," although the collection also includes maps of the Napoleonic Wars, the Chinese Civil War, the

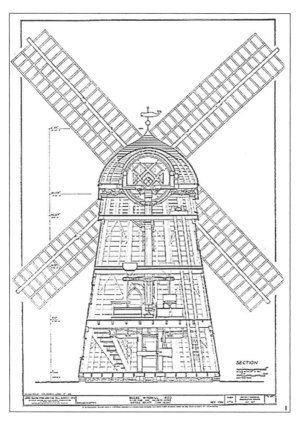

Drawing, Beebe Windmill, New York, 1968, from *Built in America: Historic American Buildings Survey and Historic American Engineering Record* [10]. *(Library of Congress, Prints and Photographs Division, Historic American Buildings Survey or Historic American Engineering Record, call number: HAER NY, 52-BRIG, 4-.)*

Falkland Islands War, and Arab-Israeli conflicts. Maps are indexed by war and may be enlarged, but are not annotated. The website is easy to navigate, although large maps may be slow to download. A bibliography lists eight atlases, published between 1959 and 1987, from which many of the maps were taken.

12. Core Historical Literature of Agriculture

Albert R. Mann Library, Cornell University
http://chla.library.cornell.edu/

Currently this website presents full-text, searchable facsimiles of 1,850 monographs and 288 journal volumes related to U.S. agriculture. All were published between 1806 and 1989. Evaluations and 4,500 core titles are detailed in the seven-volume series *The Literature of the Agricultural Sciences.* Fields of study include agricultural economics, agricultural engineering, animal science, forestry, nutrition, rural sociology,

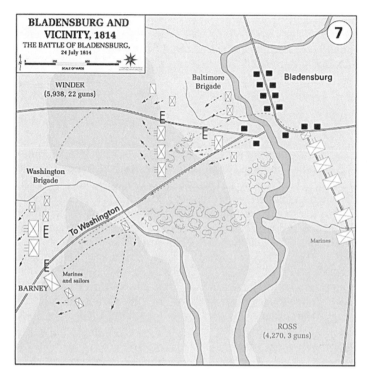

Map, Battle of Bladensburg, from *Campaign Atlases* [11]. *(United States Military Academy.)*

and soil science. Types of materials include memoirs, transactions of early agricultural societies, newspapers, almanacs, agricultural periodicals, governmental publications, and archives of families, communities, and corporations. Users can search by author, title, subject, or keyword, then access the title page, table of contents, index, or pages of the text. These resources are valuable for studying the profound social, cultural, and economic effects of shifts in the history of American farming.

13. Digital History

Steven Mintz and Sara McNeil
http://www.digitalhistory.uh.edu/

These multimedia resources for teaching American history focus on slavery, ethnic history, private life, technological achievement, and American film. There are more than 600 documents on the history of Mexican Americans, Native Americans, and slavery, from "first encounters" through the Civil War. A complete U.S. history textbook is presented, along with historical newspaper articles and more than 1,500 annotated links, including 330 links to audio files of historic speeches, and nine links to audio files of historians discussing relevant topics. Ten essays address past controversies, such as the Vietnam War, socialism, and the war on poverty. Seven essays present historical background on more recent controversies, and essays of more than 10,000 words each address the history of film and private life in America. Exhibits offer 217 photographs from a freedmen's school in Alabama and seven letters between eighteenth-century English historian Catharine Macaulay and American historian Mercy Otis Warren.

14. Digital Library of Georgia

University of Georgia Libraries
http://dlg.galileo.usg.edu/

Bringing together a wealth of material from libraries, archives, and museums, this website examines the history and culture of the state of Georgia. Legal materials include more than 17,000 state government documents from 1994 to the present, updated daily, and a complete set of Acts and Resolutions from 1799 to 1995. "Southeastern Native American Documents" provides approximately 2,000 letters, legal documents, military orders, financial papers, and archaeological images from 1730 to 1842. Materials from the Civil War–era include a soldier's diary and two collections of letters. There are eighty full-text, word-searchable versions of books from the early nineteenth century to the 1920s and three historic newspapers. Additional materials include photographs of African Americans from Augusta during the late nineteenth century; 2,500 political cartoons from 1946 to 1982; Jimmy Carter's diaries; and 1,500 architectural and landscape photographs from the 1940s to the 1980s.

15. Digital Scriptorium

Digital Scriptorium, Duke University
http://library.duke.edu/specialcollections/collections/digitized/

Embracing twelve digitized collections, five exhibits, and six student projects, this website contains a wealth of primary documents. Collections include two websites related to advertising—*Emergence of Advertising in America, 1850–1920* [122] and *Ad*Access* [185]—in addition to a collection of health-related ads from 1911 to 1958 in *Medicine and Madison Avenue* [199]. "George Percival Scriven: An American in Bohol, The Philippines, 1899–1901" presents an American officer's account of life during the occupation. "Civil War Women" offers correspondence and a diary relating to three American women of diverse backgrounds. "African American Women" presents letters by three slaves and a memoir by the daughter of slaves. "The Emma Spaulding Bryant Letters" provides ten revealing letters written in 1873 by Mrs. Bryant to her husband concerning medical and private matters. "Historic American Sheet Music" includes more than 3,000 pieces published between 1850 and 1920. "Documents from the Women's Liberation Movement" offers more than forty documents from 1969 to 1974. "William Gedney Photographs and Writings" provides close to 5,000 prints, work prints, and contact sheets from the 1950s to the 1980s. "Urban Landscapes" presents more than 1,000 images depicting urban areas.

16. Documenting the American South

University of North Carolina, Chapel Hill, Libraries
http://docsouth.unc.edu/

Nearly 1,400 documents address aspects of life in the South from the eighteenth, nineteenth, and early twentieth centuries. The database features ten major projects.

"The First Century of the First State University" presents materials on the beginnings of the University of North Carolina. "Oral Histories of the American South" offers 500 oral history interviews on civil rights as well as the environmental, industrial, and political history of the South. "First-Person Narratives of the American South, 1860–1920" provides 140 diaries, autobiographies, memoirs, travel accounts, and ex-slave narratives. *North American Slave Narratives* [93] furnishes close to 250 texts. The "Library of Southern Literature" makes available fifty-one titles in Southern literature. "The Church in the Southern Black Community, Beginnings to 1920" traces the role of the church as a central institution in African American life in the South. "The Southern Homefront, 1861–1865" documents non-military aspects of Southern life. "The North Carolina Experience, Beginnings to 1940" provides close to 600 histories, descriptive accounts, institutional reports, works of fiction, images, oral histories, and songs. "North Carolinians and the Great War" offers 170 documents on the effects of World War I and its legacy. Finally, "True and Candid Compositions: The Lives and Writings of Antebellum Students at the University of North Carolina" analyzes 121 documents written by students. Essays from the *Encyclopedia of Southern Culture* accompany all projects.

17. English Language Resources

University of Virginia, Electronic Text Center
http://etext.lib.virginia.edu/collections/languages/english/

More than 9,500 full-text works are presented here. In addition to writings by Edgar Allan Poe and Walt Whitman, there are 364 works on or by African Americans; 136 works on or by Native Americans; 467 titles by women writers; 158 titles in "Early American Fiction"; and thirty-two best sellers from 1900 to 1930. Non-literary collections include the "Jackson Davis Collection of African-American Education Photographs, 1910–1940," with nearly 6,000 images taken of black schools throughout the South by an educational reformer, and the "Philip S. Hench Walter Reed Yellow Fever Collection" of approximately 5,500 items on the conquest of the disease. The following University of Virginia "Electronic Text" websites are described elsewhere in this guide: *The Plymouth Colony Archive Project* [63], *Salem Witch Trials: Documentary Archive and Transcription Project* [66], *Thomas Jefferson Digital Archive* [80], and *Mark Twain in His Times* [129].

18. Famous Trials

Douglas Linder, Professor of Law, University of Missouri, Kansas City
http://www.law.umkc.edu/faculty/projects/ftrials/ftrials.htm

This exceptional legal history website presents balanced treatment of more than fifty prominent court trials. Trials include Salem witchcraft (1692); Burr conspiracy (1807); Amistad (1839–1840); Dakota conflict (1862); Lincoln conspiracy (1865); Johnson impeachment (1868); and Susan B. Anthony (1873). Twentieth-century trials include Bill Haywood (1907); Sacco and Vanzetti (1921); Scopes (1925); Scottsboro Boys (1931–1937); Rosenbergs (1951); Lenny Bruce (1964); "Mississippi Burning" (1967); Chicago Seven (1969–1970); My Lai courts martial (1970); LAPD officers' (1992); O. J. Simpson (1995); and Clinton impeachment (1999). Each trial website includes a chronology, maps, and court documents, including transcripts of testimony, media coverage, depositions, and government documents. Most cases also contain images, links to related websites, and a bibliography. Biographies center on five "trial heroes," including trial lawyer Clarence Darrow. "Exploring Constitutional Law" offers eighty-three topics for class discussion.

19. Florida State Archives Photographic Collection

Joan Morris, Florida State Archive
http://www.floridamemory.com/PhotographicCollection/

More than 137,000 photographs of Florida, many focusing on specific localities from the mid-nineteenth century to the present, are available on this website. The collection, including fifteen online exhibits, is searchable by subject, photographer, keyword, and date. Materials include thirty-five collections on agriculture, the Seminole Indians, state political leaders, Jewish life, family life, postcards, and tourism, among other things. Educational units address seventeen topics, including the Seminoles, the Civil War in Florida, educator Mary McLeod Bethune, folklorist and writer Zora Neale Hurston, pioneer feminist Roxcy Bolton, the civil rights movement in Florida, and school busing during the 1970s. "Writing Around Florida" includes ideas to foster appreciation of Florida's heritage. "Highlights of Florida History" presents forty-six documents, images, and photographs from Florida's Spanish period to the present. An interactive timeline presents materials—including audio and video files—on Florida at war, economics and agriculture, geography and the environment, government and politics, and state culture and history.

20. Foreign Relations of the United States (FRUS), 1861–1960

University of Wisconsin, Madison, Libraries
http://digicoll.library.wisc.edu/FRUS/

Foreign Relations of the United States, 1945–1972

U.S. State Department
http://www.state.gov/r/pa/ho/frus/c1716.htm

Published annually by the U.S. State Department, *Foreign Relations of the United States* (FRUS) is the official record of major declassified U.S. foreign policy decisions and diplomatic activity. Material, including transcripts of tape recordings, comes from presidential libraries and executive departments and agencies. Digitized material does not reflect the full range of the published volumes; documents included have been selected for their ability to illuminate "policy formulation and major aspects and repercussions of its execution." The first website covers the years from 1861 to 1960. Each volume of more than 500 pages contains an annual message from the President, a list of papers with subjects of correspondence, circulars on subjects such as sanitation and conservation, and chapters dedicated to individual nations. Decisions involve a wide range of topics, from international arbitration to the protection of migratory birds. Visitors may search volumes individually or the whole set by keyword, subject, and date. The second website offers materials from 1945 to 1972. Materials come from the Truman, Eisenhower, Kennedy, Johnson, and Nixon administrations. Additional volumes will be added on the Nixon and Ford administrations.

21. France in America

Library of Congress and Bibliothèque Nationale de France
http://international.loc.gov/intldl/fiahtml/fiahome.html

This bilingual website (English and French) explores the history of the French presence in North America from the early sixteenth century to the end of the nineteenth century through more than 360 manuscripts, books, maps, and other documents. Each thematic presentation—"Exploration and Knowledge," "The Colonies," "Franco-Indian Alliances," "Imperial Struggles," and "The French and North America after the Treaty of Paris"—includes a title exhibit and additional exhibits that highlight particular items in the collection. Materials can also be browsed in the "Collections" section. A timeline (1515–1804) organizes events in French America by explorations, colonization and development, and conflicts and diplomacy, and places them in the context of events in France. Additionally, there are eight descriptive maps that show various indigenous groups in contact with the French and the changes in political boundaries in North America from 1763 to the Louisiana Purchase.

22. Gifts of Speech: Women's Speeches from Around the World

Sweet Briar College, Virginia
http://www.giftsofspeech.org/

Charting changes in women's rhetoric in the public realm from 1848 to the present is possible through this archive of more than four hundred speeches by "influential, contemporary women." These include prominent female politicians and scientists, as well as popular culture figures. There is an emphasis on the United States, particularly after 1900, but speeches come from women as diverse as Elizabeth Cady Stanton, Sojourner Truth, Mary Church Terrell, Marie Curie, Helen Keller, Emma Goldman, Eleanor Roosevelt, Betty Friedan, and Ayn Rand. A nearly complete list of "Nobel Lectures by Women Laureates" presents acceptance speeches. The search function is particularly useful for pulling speeches from a diverse collection into common subject groups. It also allows for the study of the language of women's public debate by following changes in the use of particular metaphors or idioms, such as the concept "motherhood."

23. Gilder Lehrman Institute of American History

Gilder Lehrman Institute of American History
http://www.gilderlehrman.org

This large, attractive website provides high-quality material on American history for historians and teachers. The collection contains about 10,000 digitized American historical documents, images, and objects from 1493 to 1998, part of a larger collection of more than 60,000 items. Authors include George Washington, John Quincy Adams, Harriet Beecher Stowe, Frederick Douglass, and Abraham Lincoln. Each week, an annotated, transcribed document is featured, and an archive contains eighty documents previously featured. "Treasures of the Collection" offers twenty-four highlighted documents and images. Six online exhibits cover topics such as Alexander Hamilton, the Dred Scott decision, and Abraham Lincoln. Seven podcasts with historians address issues such as presidential history and the Great Depression. Additional resources include links to historical documents, published scholarship, and general history resources on the Web.

24. History Matters: The U.S. Survey Course on the Web

Center for History and New Media and American Social History Project/CML
http://historymatters.gmu.edu/

Providing a host of resources on U.S. history, the three main features are "WWW .History," "Many Pasts," and "Making Sense of Evidence." "WWW.History" provides an annotated guide to more than 1,000 high-quality websites covering all of U.S. history. Users can browse websites by time period or topic and can search by keyword. "Many Pasts" offers more than 1,000 primary sources in text, image, and audio, from an exchange between Powhatan and Captain John Smith to comments by the director of the Arab American Family Support Center in Brooklyn after the September 11, 2001, terrorist attacks. "Making Sense of Evidence" offers eight guides with interactive exercises designed to help students learn to analyze various kinds of primary sources, including maps, early film, oral history, and popular song. These guides offer questions to ask and provide examples of how to analyze kinds of evidence. There are also eight multimedia modules that model strategies for analyzing primary sources, including political cartoons, blues songs, and abolitionist speeches.

25. History Teacher's Bag of Tricks: Adventures in Roland Marchand's File Cabinet

Area 3 History and Cultures Project
http://marchand.ucdavis.edu/

A memorial to Roland Marchand, the late historian of popular culture and advertising, this website presents a slide library with 6,000 images, including more than 2,000 advertisements, drawn from Marchand's collection. The images are organized into forty major categories and close to 200 subcategories. The website also offers forty-eight lesson plans designed by Marchand, each with an introduction, an essay assignment, and ten to forty primary source documents. The lessons cover a diverse range of controversial topics, including the Antinomian Controversy, the Chinese Must Go!, the Pullman Strike, the Women's Suffrage Movement, and Watergate. The website will be useful for researching popular culture and advertising, as well as numerous other topics in American history, such as women, wars, immigration, labor, and African Americans.

26. Hypertext on American History from the Colonial Period until Modern Times

Professor George M. Welling, University Groningen (Netherlands), University Bergen (Norway)
http://odur.let.rug.nl/~usa/usa.htm

With more than 375 documents related to U.S. history from the colonial period to the present, this website provides important historical documents and speeches.

"Essays" contains more than thirty-five writings on various aspects of U.S. history. "Biographies" offers more than 200 biographies of historical figures related to American history, ranging from 350 words to 2,000 words in length. "Presidents" contains documents pertaining to each U.S. president, including inaugurations and State of the Union addresses. Documents and essays are hyperlinked to four editions of the booklet *An Outline of American History* (1954, 1963, 1990, and 1994), a publication distributed abroad by the U.S. Information Service, along with similar volumes on American economy, government, literature, and geography. The website provides basic primary sources for the American history survey course.

27. Images of Native Americans

Bancroft Library at the University of California, Berkeley
http://bancroft.berkeley.edu/Exhibits/nativeamericans/index.html

This collection of materials (more than eighty items) comes from rare books, pamphlets, journals, pulp magazines, newspapers, and original photographs. The illustrations reflect European interpretations of Native Americans, images of popular culture, literary and political observations, and artistic representations. The three main sections are "Portrayals of Native Americans," "The Nine Millionth Volume," and a timeline. "Portrayals" is divided into four online galleries: "Color Plate Books," "Foreign Views," "Mass Market Appeal," and "Early Ethnography." The galleries incorporate the renowned works of George Catlin and Edward S. Curtis, and the lesser-known works of early nineteenth-century Russian artist-explorer Louis Choris. "Mass Market Appeal" features thirty-two illustrations, including colorful images of western novel covers and portraits of southwestern Indians. "Early Ethnography" contains a newspaper article about a Native American family, five photographs, and fifteen illustrations of Native Americans at play and at war. "The Nine Millionth Volume" is devoted to James Otto Lewis's historic volume, *The Aboriginal Port Folio*, a series of hand-colored lithographic portraits of American Indian chiefs.

28. In Motion: The African-American Migration Experience

Schomburg Center for Research in Black Culture
http://www.inmotionaame.org/home.cfm

Migration, both forced and voluntary, remains a prominent theme in African American history. This website is built around the history of thirteen African American migration experiences: the transatlantic slave trade (1450s–1867), runaway journeys (1630s–1865), the domestic slave trade (1760s–1865), colonization and emigration (1783–1910s), Haitian immigration (1791–1809), Western migration (1840s–1970), and Northern migration (1840s–1890). Twentieth-century migrations include the Great Migration (1916–1930), the Second Great Migration (1940–1970), Caribbean immigration (1900–present), the return South migration (1970–present), Haitian immigration in the twentieth century (1970–present), and African immigration (1970–present). More than 16,500 pages of texts, 8,300 illustrations, and sixty-seven maps are included. An interactive timeline places migration in the context of U.S. history and the history of the African Diaspora.

29. Indian Affairs: Laws and Treaties

Oklahoma University Library, Digital Publications
http://digital.library.okstate.edu/kappler/

This digitized version of the book *Indian Affairs: Laws and Treaties* is a useful resource. *Indian Affairs* is a highly regarded, seven-volume compendium of treaties, laws, and executive orders relating to U.S.-Indian affairs, originally compiled by Charles J. Kappler in 1904 and updated afterward through 1970. *Volume II* presents treaties signed between 1778 and 1882. *Volumes I* and *III* through *VII* cover laws, executive and departmental orders, and important court decisions involving Native Americans from 1871 to 1970. Some volumes also provide tribal fund information. This version includes the editor's margin notations and detailed index entries, and allows searches across volumes. It provides a comprehensive resource for legal documents on U.S. relations with Native Americans.

30. Inter-University Consortium for Political and Social Research

Institute for Social Research, University of Michigan
http://www.icpsr.umich.edu/

Providing access to social science data for member colleges and universities, this website presents data that cover a range of sociological and political areas. Issues include census enumerations; urban and community studies; conflict, violence, and wars; economic behavior; legal systems; legislative bodies; mass political behavior and attitudes; and organizational behavior. While much of the website emphasizes the late twentieth century, data sets such as "Historical and Contemporary Electoral Processes" and "1790–1960 Censuses" will be useful for historical research. Searching is available according to a controlled vocabulary of names, subjects, and geographical terms. There are ten special topic archives with data geared to health, education, aging, criminal justice, and substance abuse and mental health concerns. A "data use tutorial" and links to related websites may be useful.

31. Jews in America: Our Story

Center for Jewish History
http://www.jewsinamerica.org

The history of Jews in America from the seventeenth century to the present is explored in this website through essays, images, video presentations, and interactive timelines. Eight sections focus on particular time periods: 1654–1776; 1777–1829; 1830–1880; 1881–1919; 1920–1939; 1940–1948; 1949–1967; and 1968–present. Each section has short topical essays discussing the world events, politics, and daily life of the period, video and audio presentations, an image gallery, and books for further reading. A number of sections also have "featured artifacts" that examine a particular cultural artifact, such as a colonial era book of prayers or a Civil War photo album, in greater detail. Each image is accompanied by a description and a larger size image. The 590 images in the collection can be viewed together in a gallery.

32. Kentuckiana Digital Library

Kentucky Virtual Library
http://kdl.kyvl.org/

These historical materials come from fifteen Kentucky colleges, universities, libraries, and historical societies. They include nearly 8,000 photographs; ninety-five full-text books, manuscripts, and journals from 1784 to 1971; ninety-four oral histories; seventy-eight issues of *Mountain Life and Work* from 1925 to 1962; and twenty-two issues of *Works Progress Administration in Kentucky: Narrative Reports*. Photographs include collections by Russell Lee, who documented health conditions resulting from coal industry practices; Roy Stryker, head of the New Deal Farm Security Administration photographic section; and others that provide images of cities, towns, schools, camps, and disappearing cultures. Oral histories center on Supreme Court Justice Stanley F. Reed, Senator John Sherman Cooper, the Frontier Nursing Service, veterans, fiddlers, and the transition from farming to an industrial economy. Texts include Civil War diaries, religious tracts, speeches, correspondence, and scrapbooks. Documents cover a range of topics, including colonization societies, civil rights, education, railroads, feuding, the Kentucky Derby, Daniel Boone, and a personal recollection of Abraham Lincoln.

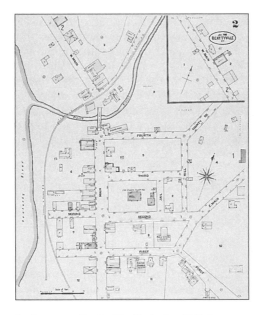

Sanborn map, Beattyville, Kentucky, 1908, from
Kentuckiana Digital Library [32]. *(Sanborn Map of
Beattyville, KY, 1908, Kentuckiana Digital Library.)*

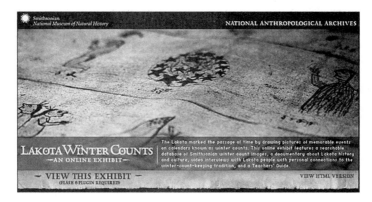

Screenshot from *Lakota Winter Counts* [33]. *(National Anthropological Archives, Smithsonian Institution.)*

33. Lakota Winter Counts

Smithsonian National Museum of Natural History
http://wintercounts.si.edu/

This anthropological exhibit displays, explains, and interprets the Lakota pictorial histories known as winter counts. Featuring a searchable database of winter count images, a documentary about Lakota history and culture, and video interviews with Lakota people, this website allows visitors to view images from ten winter counts and examine their symbols in detail by year with curator comments. Visitors are also able to examine the various symbols used by the winter count keepers to represent plants and animals, ceremonies, health, trade goods, places, people, the U.S. government, and the sky. "Who Are the Lakota" offers a historical overview of Lakota history in ten segments that include the Lakota and the Sioux people, Lakota origins, westward migration, horse-centered culture on the northern Great Plains, important conflicts and treaties, confinement to the Great Sioux Reservation, and subsequent land cessions.

34. Library of Virginia Digital Library Program

Library of Virginia
http://www.lva.lib.va.us/

More than 1.2 million items on Virginia and life in the South are available on this website, including 40,000 photographs and maps, 350,000 court documents, and 800,000 manuscripts, which include governors' letters, land office grants, Revolutionary War bounty land warrants, Confederate pensions, and disability applications. Several complete collections are available, as well as twenty-five exhibits on Virginia history. Users can find photographs that document buildings and people; patents and grants submitted to the Virginia Land Office between 1623 and 1992; Northern Neck Grants and Survey forms filed between 1692 and 1892; military records, including Revolutionary War state pensions material and World War I History Commission Questionnaires; WPA Life Histories; and Virginia Religious Petitions from 1774 to

1802. Exhibits deal with topics including the legacy of the New Deal in Virginia, resistance to slavery, Virginia roots music (with seven audio selections), Thomas Jefferson, John Marshall, Virginia's coal towns, and political life in the state.

35. Map Collections: 1500–2003

American Memory Project, Library of Congress
http://memory.loc.gov/ammem/gmdhtml/gmdhome.html

This large collection of maps from the sixteenth century to the present day focuses on Americana and "cartographic treasures." Materials are organized into seven thematic categories: "Cities and Towns," "Conservation and Environment," "Discovery and Exploration," "Cultural Landscapes," "Military Battles and Campaigns," "Transportation and Communication," and "General Maps." Sections include five special presentations. Users may download maps or zoom to view details. Seventeen specific map collections contained within this larger website that are of particular importance for the study of American history include "Discovery and Exploration," "The American Revolution and Its Era," "Railroad Maps, 1828–1900," "American Colonization Society Collection: Maps of Liberia, 1830–1870," "Panoramic Maps, 1847–1929," "Civil War Maps," and "Mapping the National Parks."

36. Museum of the City of San Francisco

Gladys Hanson, Curator
http://www.sfmuseum.org/

These eleven exhibits address the history of California and San Francisco. Topics include the Gold Rush of 1849, the earthquakes of 1906 and 1989, the history of the city's fire department, construction of the Golden Gate and Bay Bridges, and the internment of Japanese Americans during World War II. These exhibits provide timelines and links to more than 200 primary documents and images, including newspaper articles, diary entries, oral histories, photographs, political cartoons, and engravings. Two exhibits are hyperlinked chronologies pertaining to San Francisco during World War II and the rock music scene in the city from 1965 to 1969. Documents can also be accessed according to subject, with more than twenty-five documents listed on the Chinese American community, fairs and expositions, and labor issues. There are more than 150 biographies of prominent San Franciscans.

37. National Park Service: Links to the Past

National Park Service
http://www.cr.nps.gov/

Visitors to this website are invited to explore historical aspects of the roughly 200 National Park Service locations designated important to U.S. history and prehistory. Materials are organized by "cultural resource subjects," including archaeology, architecture and engineers, cultural groups, cultural landscapes, historic buildings, mapping, maritime and military history, and "cultural resource programs," such as the American Indian Liaison Program and Heritage Preservation Services. Visitors can search for information on more than 2.5 million Civil War soldiers and sailors;

more than 71,000 properties listed in the *National Register of Historic Places*; and approximately 240,000 reports on federal archaeological projects in the National Archaeological Database. "National Register Travel Itineraries" provide historic guides to eighteen cities and communities. The "National Underground Railroad Network to Freedom" contains information on fifty-one sites of importance and on slavery and antislavery efforts. Also of interest are bibliographies on the African American west and public history, and full-text publications on the Antiquities Act of 1906 and the promotion of the city of Seattle during the gold rush era. The homepage presents several comprehensive historical exhibits including the "Eisenhower Virtual Museum."

38. Naval Historical Center

U.S. Department of the Navy
http://www.history.navy.mil/

This collection addresses the history of the U.S. Navy through photographs, paintings, documents, oral histories, historical overviews, chronologies, and bibliographies. "Wars and Conflicts of the U.S. Navy" offers material on wars and naval campaigns from the Revolutionary War to Desert Storm, including oral histories from World War II. Hundreds of paintings and photographs depict U.S. Navy ships and aircraft from the early republic to the present. "African Americans and the U.S. Navy" offers images of African Americans who served from the 1860s to the 1970s. "Nurses and the U.S. Navy" provides photos and images of nurses from the nineteenth century to the 1940s. The section also offers dozens of recruiting posters and a feature with images and descriptions of U.S. Navy ships' insignia. The "Naval Art Gallery" offers twenty-four galleries including "Women in Uniform" and "The Invasion of Normandy." Additionally, the "Operational Archives Branch" offers Commander Naval Forces Vietnam (COMNAVFORV) monthly summaries from 1966 to 1973 and there are links to archives holding material on the U.S. Navy.

39. New York Public Library Digital Gallery

New York Public Library
http://digitalgallery.nypl.org/nypldigital/index.cfm

This massive collection presents more than 550,000 images relevant to both U.S. and world history, from the earliest days of print culture to the present. Resources consist primarily of historical maps, posters, prints and photographs, illuminated manuscript pages, and images drawn from published books. For browsing, the materials are divided by subject heading, library of origin, and the name of the item's creator and/or publisher. They are also sorted by collection: "Arts & Literature," "Cities & Buildings," "Culture & Society," "History & Geography," "Industry & Technology," "Nature & Science," and "Printing & Graphics." Within these broad headings, images are further subdivided into more specific groupings, such as Indonesian dance, dress and fashion, Civil War medical care, and New York City apartment buildings. All images can be downloaded and are accompanied by detailed source information, but users will have to turn elsewhere for historical context.

40. Ohio Memory: An Online Scrapbook of Ohio History

Ohio Memory Project
http://www.ohiomemory.org

This wealth of materials—more than 26,000 images in 4,100 collections—comes from 330 archives, libraries, and museums. Together, they document Ohio life, culture, and history from prehistoric times to the recent past. Currently, the website provides 2,786 visual items; 768 historical objects, artifacts, or buildings; 106 natural history specimens; 809 published works; and 691 collections of unpublished material. Users can browse or search by word, place, and subject. Displayed materials are presented chronologically on scrapbook pages with ten selections per page. "Learning Resources," with twenty-two categories, offers essays of up to 2,000 words illustrated with relevant material. Topics include African Americans, agriculture, Native Americans, arts and entertainment, business and labor, civil liberties, daily life, education, immigration and ethnic heritage, government, religion, science and technology, sports, and women.

41. Online Archive of California

University of California
http://www.oac.cdlib.org/texts

This archive provides more than 81,000 images and 1,000 texts on the history and culture of California. Images may be searched by keyword or browsed according to six categories: history, nature, people, places, society, and technology. Topics include exploration, Native Americans, gold rushes, and California events. Three collections of texts are also available. "Japanese American Relocation Digital Archive" furnishes 309 documents and sixty-seven oral histories. "Free Speech Movement: Student Protest, UC Berkeley, 1964–1965" provides 541 documents, including books, letters, press releases, oral histories, photographs, and trial transcripts. "UC Berkeley Regional Oral History Office" offers full-text transcripts of 139 interviews organized into fourteen topics including agriculture, arts, California government, society and family life, wine industry, disability rights, Earl Warren, Jewish community leaders, medicine (including AIDS), suffragists, and UC Black alumni.

42. Osher Map Library

Smith Center for Cartographic Education, University of Southern Maine
http://www.usm.maine.edu/maps/web_exhibit.html

These fourteen exhibitions include more than 600 maps and related documents on aspects of history revealed through the study of maps. The website provides well-integrated essays of up to 8,000 words for each exhibit and some annotated bibliographies. Exhibits focusing on American history include "Mapping the Republic," on conflicting conceptualizations of the United States from 1790 to 1900; "Exodus and Exiles," on Diaspora experiences of Jews and African Americans; "The American Way," a collection of twentieth-century road maps and guidebooks; "Carto-Maine-ia," on popular uses of maps; and "Maine Wilderness Transformed," that examines "the creation of a landscape of exploitation." In addition, "The Cartographic Creation of

New England" addresses European exploration and settlement; "The 'Percy Map'" presents a significant Revolutionary War map; and "John Mitchell's Map" offers insight into diplomatic disputes. These maps are especially valuable for studying exploration and cartography in American history.

43. Our Documents

National Archives and Records Administration, National History Day, and USA Freedom Corps

http://www.ourdocuments.gov

A cooperative effort, this online repository presents one hundred milestone documents in American history. The first document is the Richard Henry Lee Resolution of June 7, 1776, proposing independence for the American colonies. The last is the Voting Rights Act of 1965. In between, visitors will find Eli Whitney's 1794 cotton gin patent, the 1862 Pacific Railway Act, and the 1896 *Plessy* v. *Ferguson* ruling. Additional documents include the 1882 Chinese Exclusion Act, the Keating-Owen Child Labor Act of 1916, and orders and addresses by several presidents, including Franklin Roosevelt and Dwight Eisenhower. There is a full-page scan and transcription of each document. In addition to the chronological list of documents, the website includes a "People's Vote." Americans voted the Declaration of Independence number one, followed by the Constitution and the Bill of Rights.

44. Oyez: U.S. Supreme Court Multimedia

Jerry Goldman, Northwestern University

http://www.oyez.org/

These audio files, abstracts, transcriptions of oral arguments, and written opinions cover more than 3,300 Supreme Court cases. Materials include 3,000 hours of audio arguments in selected cases since 1955 and all cases after 1995. Users can access cases through keyword searches or a list of thirteen broad categories, such as civil rights, due process, first amendment, judicial power, privacy, and unions. Cases include *Roe* v. *Wade* (abortion), *Gideon* v. *Wainwright* (right to counsel), *Plessy* v. *Ferguson* (segregation), *Grutter* v. *Bollinger* (racial preferences in school admission decisions), and *Bush* v. *Gore* (election results). Biographies are provided for all Supreme Court justices and "The Pending Docket" provides briefs on upcoming cases. The website also includes links to opinions written since 1893 and podcasts featuring discussions of cases starting in 1793.

45. The Presidents

Kunhardt Productions and Thirteen/WNET in New York

http://www.pbs.org/wgbh/amex/presidents/index.html

All forty-three of the nation's completed presidencies are profiled in detail on this website geared toward teaching the history of the American presidency. In-depth biographies include information on childhood, education, career, elections, family life, domestic policy, and foreign affairs. Many biographies include links to numerous primary sources, such as speeches, writings, letters, and diplomatic documents. As a companion website to the PBS *American Experience* documentaries, these resources are hooked into a larger "Archives" section available at the top of the screen. Here, users will find thousands of resources, including maps, movies, and QuickTime Virtual Reality, on many topics in American history divided by theme and chronology, such as technology, popular culture, war, and urban and rural environments.

46. ProQuest Information and Learning

ProQuest Company
http://www.proquest.com

This fee-based service provides a range of resources. There is a large number of secondary sources, including more than 2,500 scholarly journals, magazines, newspapers, and trade publications, with full-text access and searching capabilities available for approximately half. Search or browse by subject on the left side of the homepage. "Newspapers Historic" offers an enormous body of primary sources, including access to the following: the *New York Times* (1851–2001), the *Washington Post* (1877–1988), the *Wall Street Journal* (1889–1986), the *Christian Science Monitor* (1908–1991), and the *Los Angeles Times* (1881–1984). For recent history, there are articles from more than 500 newspapers worldwide from the 1980s to the present; these include specialized publications from the worlds of business, education, medicine, religion, and sciences, as well as reference resources. *ProQuest* offers subscribers a variety of product "modules," so materials described above may not be available at all institutions.

47. Public Papers of the Presidency

American Presidency Project, University of California, Santa Barbara
http://www.presidency.ucsb.edu/index.php

Bringing together a wide range of material on the public communications of American presidents, as well as election data and statistical information on the office of the president, this website presents the public messages, statements, speeches, and news conference remarks of presidents from Herbert Hoover to George W. Bush. Materials can be browsed or searched by month and year. Visitors can access transcripts of all inaugural addresses and State of the Union messages, convention speeches of presidential candidates from 1960 to 2008, and all the presidential debates. The website offers major party platforms from 1840 to 2008 and transcripts of various events from the 2001 presidential transition. Transcripts from "Presidential Candidates Debates," starting in 1960, are presented. A media archive contains audio and video clips from the late nineteenth century to the present. A map shows electoral votes and popular vote totals and percentages by state from 1828 to 2008.

48. Readex Digital Collections

Newsbank
http://www.readex.com/readex/index.cfm?content=93

Hundreds of thousands of documents spanning four centuries of American history are available in this large, subscription-based archive. Broadsides, ephemera, pamphlets, and booklets are available from 1639 to 1900. More than 1,300 newspaper titles, representing all fifty states, range in date from 1690 to 1922. U.S. Senate and House of Representatives reports, journals, and other documents are available from

1817 to 1980. Legislative and executive documents from the early republic are also included. The entire body of documents is keyword searchable, and, in addition, each collection can be searched and browsed individually. These documents shed light on many aspects of American social, political, economic, and cultural history, and can provide a valuable window into the daily lives of early Atlantic peoples. The collection of broadsides and ephemera is especially useful for exploring the history of printing in the United States, as all titles can be browsed by bookseller, printer, or publisher.

49. Samuel J. May Anti-Slavery Collection

Cornell University Library
http://www.library.cornell.edu/mayantislavery/

This is one of the richest collections of anti-slavery and Civil War materials in the world. Reverend Samuel J. May, an American abolitionist, donated his collection of anti-slavery materials to the Cornell Library in 1870. Following May's lead, other abolitionists in the United States and Great Britain contributed materials. The collection now consists of more than 10,000 pamphlets, leaflets, broadsides, local anti-slavery society newsletters, sermons, essays, and arguments for and against slavery. Materials date from 1704 to 1942 and cover slavery in the United States and the West Indies, the slave trade, and emancipation. More than 300,000 pages are available for full-text searching.

50. SCETI: Schoenberg Center for Electronic Text and Image

University of Pennsylvania Special Collections Library
http://sceti.library.upenn.edu/index.cfm

This eclectic collection of more than 2,200 items spans the seventeenth to the twentieth centuries. Visitors can search material from nine sections and visit fourteen exhibitions. "A Crisis of the Union" presents 224 pamphlets, broadsides, clippings, paintings, and maps on the Civil War. A collection devoted to Theodore Dreiser presents correspondence, several editions of the novel *Sister Carrie*, an early manuscript for *Jennie Gerhardt*, and scholarly essays. More than forty audio and video recordings complement approximately 4,000 photographs from singer Marian Anderson's papers. A collection on the history of chemistry emphasizes the pre-1850 period with monographs and more than 3,000 images of scientists, laboratories, and scientific materials, while another exhibit emphasizes the ENIAC computer. Other collections on the birth of the University of Pennsylvania, early sheet music, and Jewish music and history are also available. See also *Cultural Readings: Colonization and Print in the Americas* [60].

51. Tangled Roots: A Project Exploring the Histories of Americans of Irish Heritage and Americans of African Heritage

MaryAnn Matthews and Tim O'Brien, Gilder Lehrman Center, Yale University
http://www.yale.edu/glc/tangledroots/

More than 200 documents presented here explore cultural connections between the experiences of African Americans and Irish immigrants in America. Materials relate to individual leaders; historical events; economic, political, and social factors; and cultural achievements. A section entitled "Making Connections" offers fifteen questions about historical events and people that represent the intertwined histories of Africans and Irish in America. Other topics include the end of English participation in the slave trade, the emergence of the nativist Know-Nothing Party in the 1850s, and Ku Klux Klan activities against Catholics and blacks after the Civil War. A section on "Acceptance" explores perceptions of individual and group identities and four timelines focus on displacement, oppression, discrimination, and acceptance in America. "Voices" provides a sample of thirteen public statements and interviews on ethnicity and race from ordinary modern Americans. The website also provides a bibliography; an essay by writer James McGowan, a black American with an Irish paternal grandfather; and links to related websites.

52. The Tax History Project

Tax Analysts
http://www.taxhistory.org/

Created by a non-profit group interested in "open debate on federal, state, and international tax policy," this website furnishes an eclectic range of primary and secondary resources on the history of American taxation. "Tax History Museum" currently offers a 23,000-word narrative in eight chronological segments summarizing tax policy and politics from 1660 to 1900, supplemented with seventy images and links to related documents. The twentieth-century portion is in development. "The Price of Civilization" makes available fourteen posters and more than 6,500 pages of federal documents—primarily Treasury Department reports—on the development of the current tax system during the Great Depression and World War II. "Presidential Tax Returns" includes returns of recent presidents and Vice President Cheney. "Taxing Federalism" features nine *Federalist Papers*, and "Image Gallery" offers fifteen political cartoons from the turn of the nineteenth century to 1947, many by *Washington Star* cartoonist Clifford Berryman. The website also offers a bibliography and four sound clips of federal officials discussing tax policy.

53. United States Historical Census Data Browser

Geospatial and Statistical Data Center, University of Virginia Library
http://fisher.lib.virginia.edu/collections/stats/histcensus/

Data presented here were gathered by the Inter-university Consortium for Political and Social Research from census records and other government sources. For each decade between 1790 and 1960, users can browse extensive population and economic statistical information at state and county levels, arranged according to a variety of categories, including place of birth, age, gender, marital status, race, ethnicity, education, illiteracy, salary levels, housing, and specifics dealing with agriculture, labor, and manufacturing. Users may select up to 15 variables when conducting searches and view raw data and statistical charts. Categories are inconsistent between census periods and even within particular periods, making this a rich resource for studying how census questions changed over time. The website includes a 3,750-word essay on the history of American censuses. This database is a great statistical resource for students of American history. Additional data focused on social history are available at *Integrated Public Use Microdata Series* (http://www.ipums.umn.edu/).

54. USC Archival Research Center

University of Southern California, Information Services

http://digarc.usc.edu/search/controller/index.htm

These varied collections document the history of Los Angeles and southern California. "Digital Archives" offers more than 126,000 photographs, maps, manuscripts, texts, and sound recordings in addition to exhibits. Nearly 1,200 images of artifacts from early Chinese American settlements in Los Angeles and Santa Barbara are available, as is the entire run of *El Clamor Público*, the city's main Spanish-language newspaper from the 1850s. Photographs document Japanese American relocation during World War II and photographs, documents, and oral history audio files record Korean American history. The archive also includes Works Projects Administration Land Use survey maps and Auto Club materials. A related exhibit, "Los Angeles: Past, Present, and Future," http://www.usc.edu/libraries/archives/la/, offers collections on additional topics, including discovery and settlement, California missions, electric power, "murders, crimes, and scandals," city neighborhoods, cemeteries, Disneyland, African American gangs, and the Red Car lines.

55. Women and Social Movements in the United States, 1600–2000

Thomas Dublin and Kathryn Kish Sklar

http://womhist.alexanderstreet.com/

Initially created by two history professors, this website was designed to provide "a resource and a model for teachers of U.S. Women's History." It currently offers forty-five "mini-monographs," each comprised of a background essay and relevant primary-source documents, organized around analytical questions concerning social movements. Projects are organized into five subject categories: peace and international; politics and public life; sexuality, reproduction, and women's health; work and production; and race and gender. The website includes more than 1,050 documents and 400 photographs. Now published by *Alexander Street Press* [2], it has expanded to include thousands of new documents beginning in 1600. Some materials are still available at no cost, but full access requires a fee-based subscription.

U.S. HISTORY WEBSITES BY TIME PERIOD

Three Worlds Meet and Colonization, Beginnings to 1763

56. Archive of Early American Images

John Carter Brown Library, Brown University

http://www.brown.edu/Facilities/John_Carter_Brown_Library/pages/ea_hmpg.html

The images in this collection, focusing on the Americas, come from books printed or created in Europe between about 1492 and 1825. Images include woodcuts, copper engravings, and paintings. The database, still being compiled, currently contains 4,318 images and will eventually contain 6,000. Image viewing software is available from the website. Visitors can browse the entire archive or search by time period, geographical area, keyword, or subject, including indigenous peoples, flora and fauna, artifacts, industry, human activities, geography, maps, city views and plans, and portraits. Some images, such as Ptolemy's map of the world, may be familiar. Others are reproduced for the first time. Navigation requires some practice, but is worth the effort.

57. Atlantic Slave Trade and Slave Life in the Americas: A Visual Record

Jerome Handler and Michael Tuite Jr., University of Virginia
http://hitchcock.itc.virginia.edu/Slavery/index.php

This collection of more than 1,230 images depicts the enslavement of Africans, the Atlantic slave trade, and slave life in the New World. Images are arranged in eighteen categories, including pre-colonial Africa, capture of slaves, maps, slave ships, plantation scenes, physical punishment, music, free people of color, family life, religion, marketing, and emancipation. Many of the images are from seventeenth- and eighteenth-century books and travel accounts, but some are taken from slave narratives, *Harper's Weekly*, and *Monthly Magazine*. Reference information and brief comments, often an excerpt from original captions, accompany each image. Although there is no interpretation or discussion of historical relevance, these images are valuable for learning about representations of slavery in American slave societies, especially in the Caribbean and Latin America.

58. Center for Archaeological Studies

Center for Archaeological Studies, University of South Alabama
http://www.usouthal.edu/archaeology/center.htm

Designed to showcase the work of archaeologists and their excavations at Mobile and elsewhere in Alabama, this website offers images and exhibits from several digs. Visitors can "virtually visit" archaeological sites in the town of Old Mobile, capital of the "French colony of Louisiane" from 1702 to 1711; the Mississippian Indian city of Bottle Creek (1100–1400); and the Indian fishing site of Dauphin Island Shell Mounds (1100–1550). Additional sites include the French village of Port Dauphin (1702–1725); the Dog River Plantation site, home to a French Canadian immigrant family, numerous Native Americans, and slaves (1720s–1848); and sites in downtown Mobile, including a Spanish colonial house (ca. 1800), an early nineteenth-century riverfront tavern, and antebellum cotton warehouses. "Artifacts" features more than 250 images of pottery shards with accompanying descriptions. "Great Links" presents thirty additional websites that focus on preservation, archaeology, and Alabama history. The website also includes images and information on seven additional French colonial sites in Nova Scotia, New York, Michigan, Illinois, Mississippi, and Louisiana.

59. Colonial Connecticut Records, 1636–1776

University of Connecticut Libraries

http://www.colonialct.uconn.edu/

This scanned and partially searchable version of the fifteen-volume *Public Records of the Colony of Connecticut, from April 1636 to October 1776* was originally published between 1850 and 1890. Users can search documents by date, volume, and page number. Each of the fifteen volumes, covering consecutive time periods, includes alphabetical, hyperlinked subject terms. The website also provides access by type of material: charters, documents, inventories, laws, letters, and court proceedings. Keyword searching may be available in the future, but even without this option, the website offers a wealth of accessible material on politics, legal matters, Indian affairs, military actions, social concerns, agriculture, religion, and other aspects of early Connecticut history.

60. Cultural Readings: Colonization and Print in the Americas

University of Pennsylvania Library

http://www.library.upenn.edu/exhibits/rbm/kislak/index/cultural.html

Texts about the Americas produced in Europe from the fifteenth through the nineteenth centuries are examined in this well-organized online exhibit. Over one hundred images of printed texts, drawings, artwork, and maps from published and unpublished sources are arranged into six thematic categories: "Promotion and Possession," "Viewers and the Viewed," "Print and Native Cultures," "Religion and Print," "New World Lands in Print," and "Colonial Fictions, Colonial Histories." Five scholarly essays (5,000 to 7,000 words each) contextualize the documents. A bibliography and list of links accompany the presentation. This visually attractive, thoughtfully arranged website explores connections between colonization and representation.

61. Diary, Correspondence, and Papers of Robert "King" Carter of Virginia, 1701–1732

Edmund Berkeley, Jr., University of Virginia

http://etext.lib.virginia.edu/users/berkeley/

A work-in-progress, this collection offers letters and diary entries by Robert "King" Carter (1663–1732), a wealthy landowner and leading public figure in Virginia. Educated in England, Carter inherited or acquired more than 300,000 acres in the Northern Neck Proprietary between the Rappahannock and Potomac Rivers. Carter, who owned nearly 1,000 slaves, served as a member of the Council of Virginia and as acting governor of the colony. The website presently contains transcripts of all existing Robert Carter texts, including approximately 800 letters written between 1701 and 1727, diary entries from 1722 to 1726, and wills. Each document provides both modern and original spellings, and hyperlinked notes offering identifying information for more than 130 persons, places, and things. A biography of Carter, an essay on the Northern Neck Proprietary, and a bibliography of nearly eighty titles are also available.

A

NARRATIVE

OF THE

CAPTIVITY, SUFFERINGS AND REMOVES

OF

Mrs. *Mary Rowlandson,*

Who was taken Prisoner by the INDIANS with several others, and treated in the most barbarous and cruel Manner by those vile Savages : With many other remarkable Events during her TRAVELS.

Written by her own Hand, for her private Use, and now made public at the earnest Desire of some Friends, and for the Benefit of the afflicted.

BOSTON :

Printed and Sold at JOHN BOYLE's Printing-Office, next Door to the Three Doves in Marlborough-Street. 1773.

Page from *A Narrative of the Captivity, Sufferings and Removes of Mrs. Mary Rowlandson,* in *Cultural Readings: Colonization and Print in the Americas* [60]. *(Rosenbach Museum & Library, Philadelphia, A682N. Used with permission.)*

62. The Kraus Collection of Sir Francis Drake

Library of Congress
http://international.loc.gov/intldl/drakehtml/rbdkhome.html

Sir Francis Drake, English explorer and naval strategist, made many voyages to the Americas in the late sixteenth century and circumnavigated the globe between 1577 and 1580. This collection of important primary and secondary materials about Drake's voyages in the Americas offers sixty items in various languages, including manuscripts, books, maps, medals, and portraits. Assembled by Hans Peter Kraus, a twentieth-century collector, the main presentation is Kraus's pictorial biography of Drake. The essay also features an extensive seven-part introduction by scholars David W. Waters and Dr. Richard Boulind. A timeline presents Drake's voyages with links to documents. "The Actors and Their Stage" highlights material on the key people in Drake's life, places from his voyages, and images of Drake's ship *Golden Hind* and Armada battles.

63. Plymouth Colony Archive Project

Patricia Scott Deetz, Christopher Fennell, and J. Eric Deetz, University of Virginia
http://www.histarch.uiuc.edu/plymouth/index.html

These documents and analytical essays emphasize the social history of Plymouth Colony from 1620 to 1691. This website also offers a tribute to the scholarly work of the late James Deetz, professor of historical archaeology. Documents include 135 probates, twenty-four wills, and fourteen texts containing laws and court cases on land division, master-servant relations, sexual misconduct, and disputes involving Native Americans. The website also provides more than ninety biographical studies, research papers, and topical articles that analyze "life ways" of 395 individuals who lived in the colony. It offers theoretical views on the colony's legal structure, gender roles, vernacular house forms, and domestic violence. There are twenty-five maps or plans, approximately fifty photographs, and excerpts from Deetz's books on the history and myths of Plymouth Colony and on Anglo-American gravestone styles.

64. Prairie Fire: The Illinois Country Before 1818

Prairie Fire Digitization Project and Northern Illinois University
http://dig.lib.niu.edu/prairiefire/about.html

French explorers Jacques Marquette and Louis Joliette's famed expedition landed them in Illinois Country in 1673, land occupied by Native Americans for more than a century. This website traces the history of Illinois Country from 1673 through Illinois statehood in 1818. The site is still under construction, although a wealth of primary- and secondary-source materials are currently available. More than one hundred texts and 500 images shed light on prominent themes in Illinois history: African American experience, economic development and labor, frontier settlement, law and society, politics, religion and culture, women and gender, and the Black Hawk War. A narrative history of "The Indian Experience" provides useful historical context and fifteen videos address topics such as Jesuit relations and the fur trade.

65. Raid on Deerfield: The Many Stories of 1704

Pocumtuck Valley Memorial Association (PVMA) and Memorial Hall Museum
http://1704.deerfield.history.museum

This website documents the 1704 raid on Deerfield, Massachusetts, by 300 French soldiers and their Native American allies. Visitors are introduced to the raid by a multimedia exhibit that describes white settlement patterns that led to profound cross-cultural tensions. "Explanations" includes fifteen short essays that provide historical background. "Voices and Songs" provides audio commentary for the 300th anniversary of the raid, three audio versions of Native American creation stories, and seventeenth- and eighteenth-century music. "Meet the Five Cultures" includes brief introductions to the English, French, Mohawk, Huron, and Wobanaki. Twenty-eight individual biographies include Native Americans as well as French and English

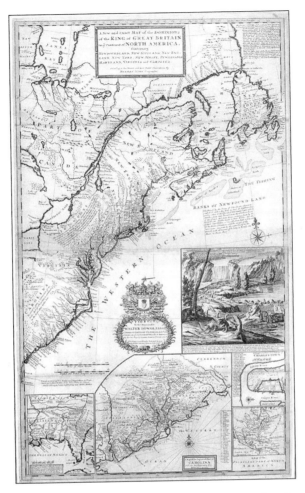

Map, Dominions of the King of Great Britain in North America, 1711, by Herman Moll, from *Raid on Deerfield: The Many Stories of 1704* [65]. *(Historic Deerfield, photo by Penny Leveritt.)*

settlers. Fourteen maps depict Native American territories and the areas involved. After viewing the evidence, visitors are asked to decide whether the raid was part of a larger pattern of cross-cultural violence or an aberration.

66. Salem Witch Trials: Documentary Archive and Transcription Project

Benjamin Ray, University of Virginia

http://etext.virginia.edu/salem/witchcraft/

This website presents a valuable collection of resources for examining the Salem Witch trials of 1692. There are full-text versions of the three-volume, verbatim Salem Witch trial transcripts, an extensive seventeenth-century narrative of the trials, and full-text pamphlets and excerpts of sermons by Cotton Mather, Robert Calef, and Thomas Maule. The website also offers four full-text rare books written in the late-seventeenth and early-eighteenth centuries about the witchcraft scare. Descriptions and images of key players in the trials are presented as well. Access is provided to more than 500 documents from the collections of the Essex County Court Archives and the Essex Institute Collection, as well as to roughly one hundred primary documents housed in other archives. There are seven maps of Salem and nearby villages. Basic information on the history of Salem/Danvers is complemented by eight related images and a brief description of fourteen historical sites in Danvers.

Illustration, "Arresting a Witch," *Harper's New Monthly Magazine,* June–November 1883, from *Salem Witch Trials: Documentary Archive and Transcription Project* [66]. *(Harper's New Monthly Magazine Vol. 67 (June–November) 1883: 221.)*

67. Slavery in New York

New York Historical Society

http://www.slaveryinnewyork.org/index.html

Focusing on the experiences of Africans and African Americans in New York City, these nine galleries explore various themes and time periods in the history of slavery. These include the Atlantic slave trade, slavery in Dutch New York, the growth of slavery in British Colonial New York, freedom for blacks during the Revolutionary War, the Gradual Emancipation Act of 1799, free blacks in public life, Emancipation Day (July 4, 1827), and the history of scholarship on slavery in New York City. Each gallery has three panels: a gallery overview, a main thematic presentation, and one focusing on people, places, and documents. Of special interest are two interactive maps with timelines in the Dutch New York gallery and the Revolutionary War gallery; a picture gallery on the portrayal of African Americans in New York City public life; and profiles of nine African Americans who lived in New York City during the early republic.

Watercolor drawing, "Indian Village of Pomeiooc," John White, 1585–1586, from *Virtual Jamestown* [68]. (© *The Trustees of the British Museum.*)

68. Virtual Jamestown

Crandall Shifflett, Virginia Center for Digital History
http://www.virtualjamestown.org

This is a good place to begin exploring the history of Jamestown. The website includes more than sixty letters and first-hand accounts from 1570 to 1720 that address voyages, settlements, Bacon's Rebellion, and early history. More than one hundred public records, such as census data and laws, fifty-five maps and images, and a registry of servants sent to plantations from 1654 to 1686 complete the website. *Virtual Jamestown* also includes records from 1607 to 1815 of Christ's Hospital in England, where orphans were trained to apprentice in the colonies. The reference section includes a timeline from 1502 to the present, narratives by prominent historians, links to twenty related websites, and a bibliography of primary and secondary sources. *The Complete Works of John Smith* and John Smith's Map of Virginia have been added to the website, while three-dimensional re-creations of Jamestown's Statehouse and Meetinghouse as well as an archive of Virginia's first Africans are being added.

Revolution and the New Nation, 1754–1820s

69. American Shores: Maps of the Middle Atlantic Region to 1850

New York Public Library
http://www.nypl.org/research/midatlantic/index.html

This attractive website explores the mid-Atlantic region and history with maps created before 1850. An extensive collection offers more than 1,852 historical maps of many different types. In addition to numerous regional and state maps, the site includes land surveys, coast surveys, nautical charts, military maps, ornamental maps, and city maps. An overview provides historical context for reading the maps of the geographic regions. The website also offers several special features. "Basics of Maps" explains such cartographic terms and features as orientation, scale, and cartouche. "Maps Through History" highlights particular maps and map genres from the collection, including a look at New York Harbor, the Hudson River, nautical charts, maps revealing early transportation routes, and maps of American Revolution battle sites. "Geographical Areas" highlights many kinds of maps and what information they offer. Visitors can click on thumbnail images to view enlarged maps and pan and zoom the maps.

70. Century of Lawmaking for a New Nation: Congressional Documents and Debates, 1774–1873

American Memory Project, Library of Congress
http://memory.loc.gov/ammem/amlaw/lawhome.html

This comprehensive set of congressional documents covers the nation's founding through early Reconstruction. Materials are organized into four categories: "Continental Congress and the Constitutional Convention," "Statutes and Documents,"

Map of North America, 1828, by Euphemia Fenno, from *American Shores: Maps of the Middle Atlantic Region to 1850* [69]. *(Permission courtesy of the New York Public Library, 1828.)*

"Journals of Congress," and "Debates of Congress." The website provides descriptions of sixteen types of documents, including bills and resolutions, *American State Papers*, the *U.S. Serial Set*, *Journals of the Continental Congress*, the *Congressional Globe*, and the *Congressional Record*. A presentation addresses the making of the Constitution and a timeline presents American history as seen in congressional documents. Special attention is directed to Revolutionary diplomatic correspondence, Indian land cessions, the Louisiana Purchase, the *Journal of the Congress of the Confederate States of America, 1861–1865*, the impeachment of Andrew Johnson, and the electoral college.

71. Do History: Martha Ballard's Diary Online

Film Study Center, Harvard University
http://dohistory.org/

This interactive case study explores the eighteenth-century diary of midwife Martha Ballard and the construction of two late twentieth-century historical studies based on the diary: historian Laurel Thatcher Ulrich's book *A Midwife's Tale* and Laurie Kahn-Leavitt's PBS film by the same name. The website provides facsimile and transcribed full-text versions of the 1,400-page diary. An archive offers images of more than fifty documents on such topics as Ballard's life, domestic life, law and justice, finance and commerce, geography and surveying, midwifery and birth, medical information, religion, and Maine history. Also included are five maps, present-day images of Augusta and Hallowell, Maine, and a timeline tracing Maine's history, the history of science and medicine, and a history of Ballard and Hallowell. The website offers suggestions on using primary sources to conduct research, including essays on reading eighteenth-century writing and probate records, searching for deeds, and exploring graveyards. A bibliography offers nearly 150 scholarly works and nearly fifty websites.

72. Documents from the Continental Congress and Constitutional Convention

American Memory Project, Library of Congress
http://memory.loc.gov/ammem/collections/continental/

These 274 sources focus on the work of the Continental Congress and the drafting and ratification of the Constitution, including manuscript annotations. The collection includes extracts of the journals of Congress, resolutions, proclamations, committee reports, and treaties. In addition, there are documents relating to the Constitutional Convention of 1787, extracts of proceedings of state assemblies and conventions relating to the ratification of the Constitution, several essays on ratification of the Constitution, and early printed versions of the U.S. Constitution and the Declaration of Independence. There are 253 titles dating from 1774 to 1788 relating to the Constitutional Congress and twenty-one dating from 1786 to 1789 relating to the Constitutional Convention. Two timelines cover the period 1764 to 1789 and an essay entitled "To Form a More Perfect Union" provides historical context for the documents through an overview of the main events of the era of the Revolution.

73. Early Virginia Religious Petitions

American Memory Project, Library of Congress
http://memory.loc.gov/ammem/collections/petitions/

This website offers images of 423 petitions submitted to the Virginia legislature between 1774 and 1802 on a variety of religious topics. The works are drawn from the Library of Virginia's Legislative Petitions Collection and represent such topics as the debate over separation of church and state, social and religious rights of Quakers, Baptists, and other dissenters, and the sale and division of property belonging to the Anglican church. Each image is accompanied by a fifteen-word caption describing the intent of the petition and the date the petition was drafted. The website also includes 200-word summaries of seventy-four other petitions that no longer exist; four images of early Virginia maps (1751–1771); a 3,000-word essay on the background, uses, and historical significance of eighteenth-century petitions; a chronology of religious developments in America from the founding of Virginia in 1607 to Alexis de Tocqueville's characterization of American religion in his *Democracy in America* (1835); links to five American Memory Project sites with related materials; and a bibliography of more than fifty related scholarly works. All can be searched by keyword and browsed by date or geographic location. These petitions are not transcribed, and some visitors may find the handwritten images difficult to read; but persistence is well worth it for those interested in religion in eighteenth-century Virginia and American cultural history.

74. First American West: The Ohio River Valley, 1750–1820

American Memory Project, Library of Congress; University of Chicago Library; and Filson Historical Society

http://memory.loc.gov/ammem/award99/icuhtml/fawhome.html

Significant European migration into the Ohio River Valley occurred from the mid-eighteenth century to the early nineteenth century and this website presents approximately 15,000 pages of materials related to this pattern. Resources include books, pamphlets, newspapers, periodicals, journals, letters, legal documents, images, maps, and ledgers. The website includes a special presentation with a 6,500-word essay on contested lands, peoples and migration, empires and politics, western life and culture, and the construction of a western past. Materials address encounters between Europeans and native peoples, the lives of African American slaves, the role of institutions such as churches and schools, the position of women, the thoughts of naturalists and other scientists, and activities of the migrants, including travel, land acquisition, planting, navigation of rivers, and trade. These are valuable resources for studying early American history, cross-cultural encounters, frontier history, and the construction of the nation's past.

75. Geography of Slavery in Virginia

Virginia Center for Digital History and Thomas Costa, University of Virginia College at Wise

http://www.vcdh.virginia.edu/gos/

Transcriptions and images of more than 4,000 newspaper advertisements for runaway slaves and indentured servants between 1736 and 1803 can be browsed or

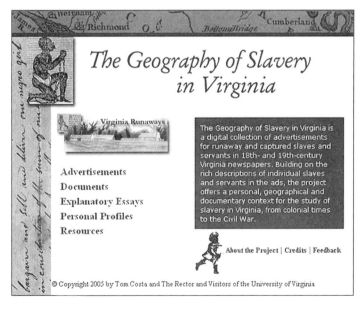

Screenshot from *Geography of Slavery in Virginia* [75]. *(Geography of Slavery website screenshot courtesy of Virginia Center for Digital History, University of Virginia [www.vcdh.virginia.edu].)*

searched on this website. The runaways are primarily from Virginia, but also come from states along the eastern seaboard and locations abroad. Materials include ads placed by owners and overseers as well as those placed by sheriffs and other governmental officials for captured or suspected runaway slaves. Additional advertisements announce runaway servants, sailors, and military deserters. "Exploring Advertisements" offers browse, search, and full-text search functions, as well as maps and timelines for viewing the geographic location of slaves. The website also provides documents on runaways—including letters, other newspaper materials, literature and narratives, and several dozen official records, such as laws, county records, and House of Burgess journals. Information on currency and clothing of the time, a gazetteer with seven maps of the region, and a thirteen-title bibliography are also available.

76. George Washington Papers, 1741–1799

American Memory Project, Library of Congress
http://memory.loc.gov/ammem/gwhtml/

This collection of approximately 152,000 documents written by or to George Washington is the largest set of original Washington documents in the world. It includes correspondence, letterbooks, diaries, journals, account books, military records, reports, and notes from 1741 through 1799. Although the website is searchable by keyword, many documents are available only as page images rather than as transcribed text and the handwriting can be difficult to read. Transcripts, however, do exist for all diary pages and for selected documents. The website includes a timeline with links to relevant documents; essays on Washington's diaries, letterbooks, and career as a surveyor and mapmaker; and an essay entitled "Creating the American Nation."

77. James Madison Papers

American Memory Project, Library of Congress
http://memory.loc.gov/ammem/collections/madison_papers/

These 12,000 items (72,000 digital images) illuminate James Madison's life, the Revolution, and the early republic. Materials include his father's letters, Madison's correspondence, personal notes, drafts of letters and legislation, and legal and financial documents. Material covers the period from 1723 to 1836. Page images of correspondence can be browsed by title, name, or correspondence series or they can be searched by keyword or phrase appearing in the bibliographic records (descriptive information) of the collection. Additionally, the full text of correspondence for which transcriptions are available can also be searched by keyword or phrase. A timeline covers the period from 1751 to 1836 and is useful for placing the events of Madison's life in historical context. Three essays are available, including one on Madison's life and papers and one on Madison at the Federal Constitutional Convention.

78. Primary Documents in American History

Library of Congress
http://www.loc.gov/rr/program/bib/ourdocs/PrimDocsHome.html

Thirty-five of the most important documents in the early history of the United States are presented here, accompanied by ample contextualization from the Library of

Page from George Washington's letterbook, 5 January 1795, in the *George Washington Papers, 1741–1799* [76]. *(Library of Congress, Manuscript Division, George Washington Papers.)*

Congress's vast collections. In addition to the "founding documents," the collection includes George Washington's Commission as Commander in Chief (1775); the *Federalist Papers* (1787–1788); the Alien and Sedition Acts (1798); the Louisiana Purchase (1803); the Missouri Compromise (1820); the Indian Removal Act (1830); the *Dred Scott* v. *Sandford* case (1857); the Emancipation Proclamation (1863); and the Thirteenth, Fourteenth, and Fifteenth Amendments to the Constitution. Each document is annotated and accompanied by a related primary-source image. Links to the American Memory Project collections and Library of Congress Exhibitions containing additional contextual documents and other secondary-source interpretations are also provided, as are links to external websites and a selected bibliography.

79. Religion and the Founding of the American Republic

Library of Congress

http://www.loc.gov/exhibits/religion/religion.html

This exhibition of 212 written documents and visual images explores the significance of religion in early American history and its relationship with the establishment of republican institutions. Materials include manuscripts, letters, books, prints, paintings, sermons, pamphlets, artifacts, and music. There are seven sections, each with a 500-word essay and item annotations. Topics include religious persecution in Europe that led to emigration, including woodcuts depicting religious violence; religious experience in eighteenth-century America, including the Great Awakening; the influence of religious leaders and ideas on the War of Independence; and evangelical movements of the early nineteenth century. Additional topics include policies toward religion of the Continental Confederation Congress, state governments, and the new federal government, including sermons and appeals that argue for and against tax-supported religion.

80. Thomas Jefferson Digital Archive

University of Virginia Library

http://etext.lib.virginia.edu/jefferson/

More than 1,700 texts written by or to Thomas Jefferson are available on this website, including correspondence, books, addresses, and public papers. While most texts are presented in transcribed, word-searchable format, eighteen appear as color images of original manuscripts. The website also includes a biography of Jefferson

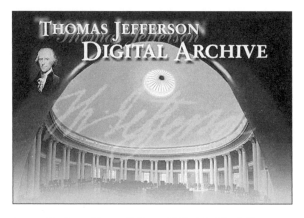

Screenshot from *Thomas Jefferson Digital Archive* [80].
(Scholar's Lab, University of Virginia Library.)

written in 1834, eight years after his death. *The Jeffersonian Cyclopedia*, published in 1900, organizes more than 9,000 quotes according to theme and other categories. A collection of 2,700 excerpts from Jefferson's writings presents his political philosophy. A wealth of searchable bibliographic listings is provided, including two previously published volumes and thousands of additional bibliographic references. Also available are a recent dissertation on the construction of the Jefferson-designed University of Virginia (UVA), listings from the *Oxford English Dictionary* that show Jefferson's influence on English language usage, and four links to UVA exhibitions on Jefferson.

81. Thomas Paine National Historical Association

Kenneth Burchell, Thomas Paine National Historical Association
http://www.thomaspaine.org/

With full-text versions of seven books and essays in addition to five nineteenth- and early twentieth-century biographies, this website presents the life and works of Thomas Paine (1737–1809). Materials include *Common Sense, The Rights of Man, The Age of Reason, The Crisis Papers,* "African Slavery in America," "Agrarian Justice," and "An Occasional Letter on the Female Sex." These texts are reproduced from *The Complete Writings of Thomas Paine,* a 1945 publication edited and annotated by historian Philip S. Foner. The website also includes Foner's section introductions and his "Chronological Table of Thomas Paine's Writings." Unfortunately, the website also includes hundreds of broken links to additional essays and letters by Paine. The biographies presented provide works published from 1819 to 1925. The website also reprints Thomas Edison's 1925 essay, "The Philosophy of Thomas Paine," in which he attempted to reawaken interest in Paine.

Expansion and Reform, 1801–1861

82. Abraham Lincoln Historical Digitization Project

Drew VandeCreek, Northern Illinois University
http://lincoln.lib.niu.edu/

This wealth of historical materials, in a variety of formats, addresses Abraham Lincoln's years in Illinois (1831–1860) and Illinois history during the same period. The website provides more than 2,300 transcriptions of documents, including correspondence, speeches, treaties, and other official papers. In addition, there are 295 images of Lincoln, his family, friends, associates, and contemporaries, as well as Illinois towns, homes, and businesses and sixty-three recordings of songs. Materials are organized into eight thematic sections: "African-American Experience and American Racial Attitudes," "Economic Development and Labor," "Frontier Settlement," "Law and Society," "Native American Relations," "Politics," "Religion and Culture," and "Women's Experience and Gender Roles." Each theme includes a background essay, relevant documents and images, video discussions by prominent historians, and narrated slide shows. "Lincoln's Biography" divides his life into eight segments with a summary and biographical text by scholars, as well as a bibliography.

Sketch, Lincoln-Douglas debate, 1858 election, from the *Abraham Lincoln Historical Digitization Project* [82]. *(University of Chicago Library, Special Collections Research Center.)*

83. Accessible Archives

Accessible Archives
http://www.accessible.com

These eight databases present more than 176,000 articles from nineteenth-century newspapers, magazines, books, and genealogical records. Much of the material comes from Pennsylvania and other mid-Atlantic states. *Godey's Lady's Book* (1830–1880), one of the most popular nineteenth-century publications, furnished middle- and upper-class American women with fiction, fashion, illustrations, and editorials.

The *Pennsylvania Gazette* (1728–1800), a Philadelphia newspaper, is described as "The *New York Times* of the Eighteenth Century." "The Civil War: A Newspaper Perspective" includes major articles from the *Charleston Mercury*, the *New York Herald*, and the *Richmond Enquirer*. "African American Newspapers: The Nineteenth Century" includes runs from six newspapers published in New York, Washington, D.C., and Toronto between 1827 and 1876. "American County Histories to 1900" provides sixty volumes covering the local history of New Jersey, Delaware, and Pennsylvania. "The Pennsylvania Genealogical Catalogue: Chester County 1809–1870" has been partially digitized, with 25,000 records available. "The Pennsylvania Newspaper Record: Delaware County 1819–1870" addresses industrialization in a rural area settled by Quaker farmers.

84. America's First Look into the Camera: Daguerreotype Portraits and Views, 1839–1864

American Memory Project, Library of Congress
http://memory.loc.gov/ammem/daghtml/daghome.html

Produced at the Mathew Brady studio, this collection contains more than 725 early photographs, most of them daguerreotypes. The Brady images include portraits of prominent public figures, such as President James K. Polk, Thomas Hart Benton, Thomas Cole, Horace Greeley, and the earliest known images of President Abraham Lincoln and his wife Mary Todd Lincoln. In addition, the website presents daguerreotypes by African American photographers; architectural views taken around Washington, D.C., and Baltimore, MD; street scenes of Philadelphia, PA; early portraits by Robert Cornelius; and copies of painted portraits. A short introduction to the daguerreotype medium and a "Timeline of the Daguerrian Era" provide context for the images. A special presentation, "Mirror Images: Daguerreotypes at the Library of Congress," includes photographs from the American Colonization Society, occupational daguerreotypes, portraits, and architectural views. These resources are especially useful for studying nineteenth-century photography and visual culture, as well as for viewing some of the earliest American photographs.

85. American Transcendentalism Web

Ann Woodlief, Virginia Commonwealth University
http://www.vcu.edu/engweb/transcendentalism/

This comprehensive collection presents texts by and about the major figures of American Transcendentalism, a New England intellectual movement that began in the mid-1830s and lasted into the late 1840s. The movement has had a much longer legacy, however, in American literature, philosophy, religion, and political and social reform. Some materials are available on the website; others are provided through links. Eleven major authors are featured: Ralph Waldo Emerson, Henry David Thoreau, Margaret Fuller, Dr. William Ellery Channing, his son William Ellery Channing, Theodore Parker, Amos Bronson Alcott, Jones Very, Christopher Cranch, Orestes Brownson, and Elizabeth Palmer Peabody. Texts are also retrievable according to themes and genre. Resources include more than one hundred selections from *The Dial*, a journal created by the Transcendentalist Club in 1840 that lasted for four years, and informative essays that provide a historic overview.

Photograph of a Liberian senator from *America's First Look into the Camera: Daguerreotype Portraits and Views, 1839–1864* [84]. *(Library of Congress, Prints & Photographs Division, reproduction number LC-USZ6-1933 DLC.)*

86. Dred Scott Case

Washington University Libraries, St. Louis
http://library.wustl.edu/vlib/dredscott/

Facsimiles and transcriptions of eighty-five legal documents relating to the Dred Scott case are provided on this website. The case began in 1846 when slaves Dred and Harriet Scott sued for their freedom, basing their argument on the fact that they had lived in non-slave territories for a number of years. The case ended with the landmark U.S. Supreme Court decision of 1857 that not only denied Scott both citizenship and the right to sue in federal court, but ruled that he never had been free and that Congress did not have the right to prohibit slavery in the territories. The decision sparked increased sectional tensions in the years leading to the Civil War. The website also provides a chronology and links to 301 "Freedom Suits," legal petitions for freedom filed by or on behalf of slaves, in St. Louis courts from 1814 to 1860.

87. Edgar Allan Poe

Edgar Allan Poe Society of Baltimore
http://www.eapoe.org/

Knowing Poe

Maryland Public Television
http://knowingpoe.thinkport.org/default_flash

Annotated versions of almost all material published by Poe during his lifetime (1809–1849) are presented on these two websites, including at least one example of all surviving poems and tales. In many cases multiple versions are provided. Materials include selections of Poe's literary reviews and essays on a variety of subjects, including aesthetics, dreams, etiquette, and American literature. Also available are autobiographical writings, hundreds of letters, and miscellaneous documents, including a bill of sale for a slave. Bibliographies and an annotated chronology are also available. The website *Knowing Poe* provides a more interactive examination of the life and death of Edgar Allan Poe. The interactive "It'll Be the Death of Me" section walks visitors through the various explanations of Poe's mysterious death. "Point of View" uses Poe's short story "The Cask of Amontillado" to illustrate the effect of point-of-view in literature; viewers can choose to read the story from the point of view of Fortunato, Montresor, or a narrator. For Poe's poem "The Bells," visitors control the voice of the reader (male or female, emotive or monotonic), add or delete sound effects and background music, and then listen to the creation to see how those factors affect the emotional impact of poetry.

88. Immigration to the United States, 1789–1930

Harvard University Library Open Collections Program
http://ocp.hul.harvard.edu/immigration/

This site includes selected historical materials focusing on voluntary immigration to the United States. The collection contains approximately 1,800 books and pamphlets, 9,000 photographs, 200 maps, and 13,000 pages from manuscript and archival collections, including diaries, biographies, and other personal writings. A timeline includes links to primary sources. Contextual information on voluntary immigration with quantitative data, as well as links to related digital resources covering other aspects of American immigration and the African diaspora fill out this site. Search capabilities allow viewers to browse by subject or genre or do a keyword or an advanced search. The primary-source interface is very easy to use and easy to navigate, with digital images, searchable text versions, and various printing capabilities. Selections come from Harvard's libraries, archives, and museums and draw heavily from the nineteenth century.

89. Journals of the Lewis and Clark Expedition

University of Nebraska Press; Center for Great Plains Studies; UNL Libraries
http://lewisandclarkjournals.unl.edu/

This well-designed website presents the "celebrated Nebraska edition of the Lewis and Clark journals," edited by Gary E. Moulton. The complete text of all the journals from the 1803 to 1806 expedition is available, along with introductions, prefaces, and sources. The material is searchable by keyword and phrase. There are twenty-nine scholarly essays about the expedition. An image gallery offers 124 images of pages from the journals, ninety-five images of people and places, and fifty images of plants and animals encountered on the expedition. The maps section includes twelve explanatory maps and nine maps from the journals. Additionally, there are twenty-seven audio excerpts of journal readings and eight video interviews with the editor of the project.

90. Lester S. Levy Collection of Sheet Music

Milton S. Eisenhower Library, Johns Hopkins University
http://levysheetmusic.mse.jhu.edu/index.html

Scanned images of more than 18,000 pieces of sheet music, including covers, published prior to 1923 are presented on this website. The collection, compiled by an

Sheet music, Irving Berlin, from the *Lester S. Levy Collection of Sheet Music* [90]. *(The Lester S. Levy Collection of Sheet Music, Special Collections, Sheridan Libraries, Johns Hopkins University.)*

American musicologist, covers the period 1780 to 1980 but focuses on nineteenth-century popular music, especially songs relating to military conflicts, presidents, romance, transportation, and songs from the minstrel stage. Users may search for songs on hundreds of topics such as drinking, smoking, fraternal orders, the circus, and death, or look for composers, song titles, or other catalog record data. Descriptions by the collector of significant songs in thirty-eight topical categories are also available. These materials are useful for studying nineteenth- and early twentieth-century popular culture, especially depictions of ethnicity, gender, and race.

91. Mexican-American War and the Media

Professor Linda Arnold, Virginia Tech University
http://www.history.vt.edu/MxAmWar/index.htm

These more than 5,500 transcribed newspaper articles related to the Mexican-American War represent five newspapers from the United States and England. They span the period from 1845, when the United States annexed Texas, through 1848, when Mexico surrendered and the Treaty of Guadalupe Hidalgo was signed. The contrast between coverage of the war in the United States and England is particularly striking. *The Times* of London fulminated against the immorality of slavery and of the Southern scheme to annex Texas as a slave state, while exposing America's imperialist ambitions as, among other things, an attempt to shore up the nation's fragile stability through the escape valve of western migration. By contrast, newspapers from Maryland and West Virginia did not examine the issue of slavery in the articles included here. Some images and links to watercolor and print collections are also available. The website provides a comprehensive bibliography on the war, but offers little historical background or contextualization beyond links to related materials and an expanded timeline.

92. Nineteenth-Century American Children and What They Read

Pat Pflieger
http://www.merrycoz.org/kids.htm

This website is devoted to the examination of nineteenth-century children in America: what they read, what was written about them, and what was written for them. "Children" includes letters, adoption advertisements, paper rewards for obedient children, twenty-four contemporary articles for and about children, and fourteen photographs, as well as scrapbooks and exercise books. "Magazines" features illustrations, articles, editorials, and letters from twelve different children's magazines, with cover and masthead images from 173 different volumes. "Books" includes twenty-two articles on children and reading (including one warning children to avoid mental gluttony by not reading too much), and the full text of twenty-nine books, including the *American Spelling Book* and grammar primers. Although the website is not searchable, the documents are indexed and arranged by subject. The website includes eight analytical essays written by modern scholars, a timeline covering the years 1789 to 1873 (with entries covering subjects like magazines, books, historical events, and people), and eight separate bibliographies. A "puzzle drawer" includes word games played by nineteenth-century children.

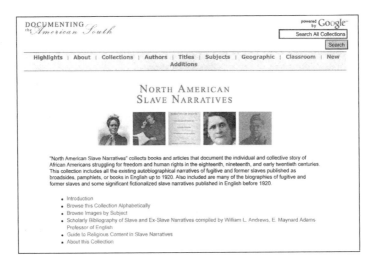

Screenshot from *North American Slave Narratives, Beginnings to 1920* [93].
(Digital Publishing Group, University of North Carolina Digital Library & Archives.)

93. North American Slave Narratives, Beginnings to 1920

William Andrews, University of North Carolina at Chapel Hill
http://docsouth.unc.edu/neh/

Offering 230 full-text documents, this collection presents the written lives of American slaves, including all known published slave narratives and many published biographies of slaves. Materials include autobiographical narratives of fugitive and former slaves published in a range of formats, such as broadsides, pamphlets, and books. In addition, biographies of fugitive and former slaves and fictionalized slave narratives are included. The collection includes well-known authors, such as Sojourner Truth and Frederick Douglass, as well as many authors less commonly known. Documents are available in HTML and SGML/TEI file formats and are accessible through alphabetical and chronological listings. Users can also view images of the covers, spines, title pages, and versos of title pages. Documents are indexed by subject, but searches return materials in additional collections. An introductory essay by Professor of English William Andrews is also available.

94. Rivers, Edens, Empires: Lewis and Clark and the Revealing of America

Library of Congress
http://www.loc.gov/exhibits/lewisandclark/lewisandclark.html

Thomas Jefferson outlined three motivating factors in his instructions to Lewis and Clark: a search for navigable rivers to span the continent, a quest for Edenic beauty and riches, and the competitive desire to acquire a continental empire. These 180 documents and artifacts interpret nineteenth-century westward exploration from this perspective. The range of materials is striking. In addition to maps, plans, and charts, the website offers images (sketches, watercolors, etchings, and engravings), texts (letters, diaries, speeches, newspapers, and books), and tools (surveying and medical instruments, cooking utensils, armaments). The exhibit opens with an examination of the "imperial mentality" common to Virginia's aristocratic class in the late eighteenth century and then focuses on the Lewis and Clark journey. It ends with the subsequent expeditions of Zebulon Pike, Stephen H. Long, Charles Wilkes, John Charles Fremont, and the mid-nineteenth century transcontinental railroad plan that supplanted the search for a water route.

95. Slaves and the Courts, 1740–1860

American Memory Project, Library of Congress
http://memory.loc.gov/ammem/sthtml/sthome.html

More than one hundred published materials on legal aspects of slavery are available on this website. These include 8,700 pages of court decisions and arguments, reports, proceedings, journals, and a letter. Most of the pamphlets and books pertain to American cases in the nineteenth century. The website features courtroom proceedings from famous trials such as the eighteenth-century *Somerset* v. *Stewart* case in England, the Amistad case, the Denmark Vesey conspiracy trial, and trials of noted abolitionists John Brown and William Lloyd Garrison. Additional documents address the slave trade, slave codes, the Fugitive Slave Law, and slave insurrections. A special presentation discusses the slave code in the District of Columbia. Searchable by keyword, subject, author, and title, this website is valuable for studying legal history, African American history, and nineteenth-century American history.

96. Sunday School Books: Shaping the Values of Youth in
Nineteenth-Century America

American Memory Project, Library of Congress; Michigan State University Libraries; and Central Michigan University
http://memory.loc.gov/ammem/collections/sundayschool/

These full-text transcriptions and page images of 163 "Sunday school books" address religious instruction for youth published in the United States between 1815 and 1865. Materials include texts used by Methodists, Baptists, Mormons, and other denominations and are searchable by subject, author, title, and keyword. Books are categorized according to several topics, including "Advice Books," "Moral Tales," "Animals, Natural History," "Child Labor, Orphans, Poverty," "Death, Dying, Illness," "Holidays," "Immigrants," "Slavery, African Americans, Native Americans," "Temperance, Tobacco," and "Travel, Missionaries." There are sixty-seven author biographies and an essay on Sunday school books. This collection offers valuable materials for studying antebellum culture, American religious history, print culture, and education.

97. Trails to Utah and the Pacific: Diaries and
Letters, 1846–1869

American Memory Project, Library of Congress; Brigham Young University; and Utah Academic Library Consortium
http://memory.loc.gov/ammem/award99/upbhtml/overhome.html

Diaries documenting the westward treks of forty-five men and four women during the period of the California Gold Rush and the westward migration of Mormonism are presented on this website. Although most of these travelers took either the California or Mormon trails, a few diaries provide accounts describing life on trails to Oregon and Montana. The diaries are complemented by eighty-two photographs and illustrations, and forty-three maps, including an interactive map displaying trails, cities, rivers, and landmarks. There are seven published guides, two essays on the Mormon and California trails, brief biographies of most of the diarists, and a list of suggested readings. This is an excellent collection of materials that documents forty-nine individual perspectives on a movement that encompassed an estimated 500,000 people.

Civil War and Reconstruction, 1850–1877

98. Abraham Lincoln Papers

American Memory Project, Library of Congress and Lincoln Studies Center, Knox College

http://memory.loc.gov/ammem/alhtml/malhome.html

Approximately 20,000 documents relating to President Abraham Lincoln's life and career are offered on this website. All of the materials are available as page images and about half have been transcribed. Resources include correspondence, reports, pamphlets, and newspaper clippings. While the documents date from 1833 to 1897, most material was written between 1850 and 1865, including drafts of the Emancipation Proclamation and Lincoln's second inaugural address. A chronological index offers names of correspondents and document titles. Special presentations on the Emancipation Proclamation and the Lincoln assassination provide introductions, timelines, and twenty-four images of related documents and engravings. Additional resources include sixteen photographs of the Lincolns and key political and military figures of Lincoln's presidency. This is an excellent resource for researching Lincoln's presidency and American politics prior to and during the Civil War.

99. Born in Slavery: Slave Narratives from the Federal Writers' Project, 1936–1938

American Memory Project, Library of Congress

http://lcweb2.loc.gov/ammem/snhtml/snhome.html

More than 2,300 first-hand accounts of slavery and 500 black and white photographs of former slaves are presented on this website. These materials were collected in the 1930s by the Federal Writers' Project of the Works Project Administration, a Roosevelt administration New Deal bureau. Each slave narrative transcript and photograph is accompanied by notes including the name of the narrator, place and date of the interview, interviewer's name, length of transcript, and catalog information. Browse photographs and narratives by keyword, subject, and narrator. An introductory essay discusses the significance of slave narratives and a selection of excerpts from eight narratives along with photographs of the former slaves. This is a rich resource for exploring slavery, historical memory, and New Deal efforts to document America's past.

Photograph, Lucindy Lawrence Jurdon, Alabama, 1936–1938,
from *Born in Slavery: Slave Narratives from the Federal
Writers' Project, 1936–1938* [99]. *(Library of Congress, Prints &
Photographs Division, Digital ID number, mesnp 010242.)*

100. Civil War Treasures from the New York Historical Society

American Memory Project, Library of Congress and New York Historical Society
http://memory.loc.gov/ammem/ndlpcoop/nhihtml/cwnyhshome.html

More than 1,500 items pertaining to the Civil War are available on this website, such as letters, newspapers, photographs, sketches, etchings, and posters. Manuscript materials include items from the papers of social reformer William Oland Bourne, a newspaper created by Confederate prisoners, three letters by Walt Whitman, and thirty-two letters by a nurse at a federal prison camp hospital. The website contains sketches dealing with the New York City Draft Riot of 1863, drawings of army life by artists working for *Frank Leslie's Illustrated Newspaper*, and a Confederate prisoner's sketchbook. Additional materials include 731 stereographs and more than seventy albumen photographs, approximately 500 envelopes with decorative materials, twenty-nine caricatures by a German immigrant in Baltimore sympathetic to the Confederacy, and 304 posters, most of which were used for recruiting purposes.

101. Freedmen's Bureau Online

Christine's Genealogy Websites, Inc.
http://www.freedmensbureau.com/

The Bureau of Refugees, Freedmen, and Abandoned Lands, also known as the Freedmen's Bureau, was established by the War Department in 1865 to supervise all relief and education activities for refugees and freedmen after the Civil War. The Bureau was responsible for issuing rations, clothing, and medicine, and had custody of confiscated lands in the former Confederate states and other designated territories. This website contains an extensive collection of Freedmen's Bureau records and reports. Included are more than one hundred transcriptions of reports on murders, riots, and "outrages" (any criminal offense) that occurred in the former Confederate states from 1865 to 1868. There are also thirty links to records and indexes of labor contracts between freedmen and planters between 1865 and 1872; seven links to related websites; six links to marriage records of freedmen, 1861 to 1872; and more than one hundred miscellaneous state record items concerning freedmen.

102. Historical *New York Times* Project— The Civil War Years, 1860–1866

University Library, Carnegie Mellon University
http://www.nyt.ulib.org/index.cgi

Designed to provide access to the *New York Times* for the Civil War years, this website includes reproductions of all pages from 1860 through 1866. For the war years, more than eighty significant articles are arranged chronologically by year. They are also arranged by topic, including battles, military, politics, relations among the states, and social issues. Articles deal with Lincoln's election, inauguration, and assassination; press censorship; abolition of slavery; formation of the Confederate States of America; and Sherman's March to the Sea, among other topics. Presently, twenty-three articles are available that detail the war's aftermath, and there are plans to add more for the years following 1866. In addition, users can select any page for any issue published during the decade. Additional material is available for the years 1900 to 1907. Full-text access to the newspaper's complete run is available through the subscription service *ProQuest* [46].

103. Lost Museum

ASHP/CML and New Media Lab, CUNY and CHNM, George Mason University
http://www.lostmuseum.cuny.edu/

P. T. Barnum's American Museum burned down under mysterious circumstances in 1865 after nearly a quarter century of patronage. The original museum tried to both entertain and educate with exhibits on natural history, American history, and reform efforts, along with attractions of a sensational nature. With the exception of African

Americans, who were barred from entry until the Civil War, New Yorkers of diverse ethnic, gender, and class identities mingled in the museum's shared cultural space. Visitors to this website can explore an interactive three-dimensional re-creation of the museum or an archive of images, documents, accounts, and essays on sixteen original Barnum exhibits, including the Fejee mermaid; Joice Heth, a former slave advertised as George Washington's nursemaid; "Swedish Nightingale" Jenny Lind; John Brown; Jefferson Davis; the Lincoln assassination; the Civil War in New York; and phrenology. The website allows visitors to immerse themselves in the popular culture of Barnum's era.

104. Selected Civil War Photographs

American Memory Project, Library of Congress

http://memory.loc.gov/ammem/cwphtml/cwphome.html

More than 1,000 photographs depict Civil War military personnel, preparations for battle, and the aftermath of battles in the main eastern theater and in the west. Photographs also include Federal Navy and Atlantic seaborne expeditions against the Confederacy, Confederate and Union officers and enlisted soldiers, and Washington, D.C., during the war. Most images were created under the supervision of photographer Mathew B. Brady. Additional photographs were taken by Alexander Gardner after leaving Brady's employment to start his own business. The presentation "Time Line of the Civil War" places images in historical context. "Does the Camera Ever Lie?" demonstrates the constructed nature of images, showing that photographers sometimes rearranged elements of their images to achieve a more controlled effect. This website is useful for studying nineteenth-century American photography and Civil War history.

Photograph, defenses of Washington, Arlington House, 1864, from *Selected Civil War Photographs* [104]. *(Library of Congress, Prints & Photographs Division, reproduction number LC-DIG-cwpb-03890 DLC.)*

105. Territorial Kansas Online

Kansas State Historical Society and University of Kansas

http://www.territorialkansasonline.org/cgiwrap/imlskto/index.php

These collections convey the growing divisions in Kansas and the nation over the expansion of slavery, federalism, nationalism, industrialization, and changing political coalitions in Congress. Materials include government documents, diaries, letters, photographs, maps, newspapers, rare secondary sources, historical artifacts, and images of historic websites. The website is divided into five sections: "Territorial Politics and Government," "Border Warfare," "Immigration and Early Settlement," "Personalities," and "National Debate About Kansas." Each is searchable by keyword, author, and county. Topical sections are subdivided into relevant themes and include an introductory essay. Visitors will find essays on territorial politics, the rights of women and African Americans, military organizations, and free state and pro-slavery organizations. "Personalities" lists thirty-two individuals, including John Calhoun, and the final section presents both anti-slavery and pro-slavery perspectives of the national debate about Kansas. The website also includes a timeline with links and an annotated bibliography.

Page, Kansas-Nebraska Act, 1854, from *Territorial Kansas Online* [105].
(National Archives and Records Administration, Washington, D.C.)

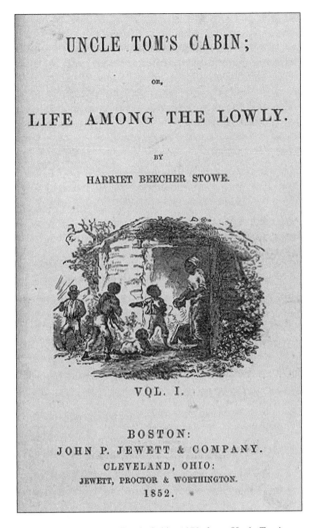

Title page from *Uncle Tom's Cabin*, 1852, from *Uncle Tom's Cabin and American Culture* [106]. *(Uncle Tom's Cabin, Special Collections, University of Virginia Library.)*

106. Uncle Tom's Cabin and American Culture

Stephen Railton, University of Virginia
http://jefferson.village.virginia.edu/utc/

This well-designed, comprehensive website explores Harriet Beecher Stowe's *Uncle Tom's Cabin* "as an American cultural phenomenon." "Pre Texts, 1830–1852" provides dozens of texts, songs, and images from the various genres Stowe drew upon, including Christian texts, sentimental culture, anti-slavery texts, and minstrel shows. The section on the novel includes Stowe's preface, multiple versions of the text, playable songs from the novel, and Stowe's defense against criticism. A third section focuses on responses from 1852 to 1930, including twenty-five reviews, more than four hundred articles and notes, as well as nearly one hundred responses from African Americans and almost seventy from pro-slavery adherents. "Other Media" explores theatrical and film versions, children's books, songs, poetry, and games. Fifteen interpretive exhibits challenge users to investigate how slavery and race were defined and redefined as well as analyze how various characters assumed a range of political and social meanings.

107. Union Army Project

Center for Population Economics, University of Chicago;
Department of Economics, Brigham Young University
http://www.cpe.uchicago.edu/unionarmy/unionarmy.html

These medical and mortality statistics and records relate to 35,747 white males who served in the Union Army during the Civil War who were later eligible for federal pensions. These materials are part of a larger study attempting to create "life-cycle datasets" to explore the effects of lifestyle and biomedical interventions on the human life span. The website presents three datasets based on different sources of information: military, pension, and medical records. These are compiled from wartime and pension application records; surgeon's certificates, with information from detailed physical examinations; and census records from 1850, 1860, 1900, and 1910. Individual soldiers were tracked through various data sources with unique Army identification numbers. The website includes a 2,000-word essay that discusses the scientific and historical background for the study and a 700-word summary of significant results.

108. Valley of the Shadow: Two Communities in the American Civil War

Edward L. Ayers, Anne S. Rubin, William G. Thomas, University of Virginia
http://valley.vcdh.virginia.edu/

This massive, searchable archive compares two Shenandoah Valley counties during the Civil War period—Augusta County, Virginia, and Franklin County, Pennsylvania. These two counties were divided by 200 miles and the institution of slavery. Thousands of pages of maps, images, letters, diaries, and newspapers, in addition to church, agricultural, military, and public records, provide data, experiences, and perspectives from the eve of the war until its aftermath. The website furnishes timelines, bibliographies, and other materials intended to foster research into the Civil War and the lives of those affected by it. The website includes a section on John Brown, http://jefferson.village.virginia.edu/jbrown/master.html, and one entitled "Memory of the War," presenting postwar writings on battles, the lives of soldiers, reunions, obituaries and tributes, and politics.

109. Wright American Fiction, 1851–1875

Committee on Institutional Cooperation; Indiana University Digital Library Program
http://www.letrs.indiana.edu/web/w/wright2/

An ambitious attempt to digitize nineteenth-century American fiction as listed in Lyle Wright's bibliography, *American Fiction, 1851–1875,* this collection of texts is a work-in-progress. At present, the website offers close to 3,000 texts by 1,456 authors. These include the well known, such as Louisa May Alcott and Mark Twain, as well as hundreds of lesser-known authors. Topics include slavery, reform, education, politics, love, children, and war. Close to 800 have been fully edited and SGML encoded so that users may access chapter and story divisions through table of contents hyperlinks. The remaining texts can be read either as facsimiles of original pages or in unedited transcriptions. The ability to perform single word and phrase searches on all material in the database—whether fully encoded or not—is powerful.

Development of the Industrial United States, 1870–1900

110. African-American Experience in Ohio:
Selections from the Ohio Historical Society

American Memory Project, Library of Congress and Ohio Historical Society
http://memory.loc.gov/ammem/award97/ohshtml/aaeohome.html

The collection includes more than 30,000 items relating to African American life in Ohio between 1850 and 1920, including personal papers, association records, a plantation account book, ex-slave narratives, legal records, pamphlets, and speeches. More than 15,000 articles from eleven Ohio newspapers and the *African Methodist Episcopal Church Review*, perhaps the oldest African American periodical, are included. The website also provides more than 300 photographs of local community leaders, buildings, ex-slaves, and African American members of the military and police. Materials represent themes such as slavery, abolition, the Underground Railroad, African Americans in politics and government, and religion. Items include an extensive collection of correspondence by George A. Myers, an African American businessman and politician, as well as prominent political speeches.

111. African American Perspectives: Pamphlets from
the Daniel A. P. Murray Collection, 1818–1907

American Memory Project, Library of Congress
http://memory.loc.gov/ammem/aap/aaphome.html

Nineteenth-century African American pamphlets and documents, most produced between 1875 and 1900, are presented on this website. These 350 works include sermons, organization reports, college catalogs, graduation orations, slave narratives, congressional speeches, poetry, and play scripts. Topics cover segregation, civil rights, violence against African Americans, and the African colonization movement. Authors include Frederick Douglass, Booker T. Washington, Ida B. Wells-Barnett, Benjamin W. Arnett, Alexander Crummel, and Emanuel Love. Publication information and short content descriptions accompany each pamphlet. The website also offers a timeline of African American history from 1852 to 1925 and reproductions of original documents and illustrations. A special presentation, "The Progress of a People," re-creates a meeting of the National Afro-American Council in December 1898. This is a rich resource for studying nineteenth- and early twentieth-century African American leaders and representatives of African American religious, civic, and social organizations.

Screenshot from *African American Women Writers of the Nineteenth Century* [112]. *(Permission courtesy of the New York Public Library.)*

112. African American Women Writers of the Nineteenth Century

Digital Schomburg: The New York Public Library
http://digital.nypl.org/schomburg/writers_aa19/

These fifty-two published works by black women writers are from the late eighteenth century through the early twentieth. The full-text database offers works by late eighteenth-century poet Phillis Wheatley, late nineteenth-century essayist and novelist Alice Dunbar-Nelson, and Harriet Jacobs, a woman born into slavery who published her memoirs, *Incidents in the Life of a Slave Girl*, in the late nineteenth century. Users can browse by title, author, or type of work (fiction, poetry, biography and autobiography, and essays). Each browse category also contains a keyword search for subjects such as religion, family, and slavery. Brief biographies of the thirty-seven featured writers are available. This website is easy to use and is ideal for learning about African American history, women's history, and nineteenth-century American literature.

113. Alexander Graham Bell Family Papers

American Memory Project, Library of Congress
http://memory.loc.gov/ammem/bellhtml/bellhome.html

The papers of telephone inventor Alexander Graham Bell (1847–1922), more than 4,600 items, are presented on this website. Materials include family papers, general correspondence, laboratory notebooks from 1891 to 1893 and 1910, scientific notebooks, blueprints, journals, articles, lectures, and photographs. Writings address a range of subjects, including the telephone, deaf education, experiments with aeronautics, and other inventions. There are more than one hundred letters to and from Helen Keller, family correspondence, and material on life in Washington, D.C., and Nova Scotia, where Bell had a summer home and conducted experiments. Ten "collection highlights," including notebook pages, document his first success with the telephone. The website also includes essays on Bell's career and on the telephone, an annotated timeline, a nineteen-title bibliography, and a list of related websites.

Photograph, Indian baskets, Washington, 1900, from *American Indians of the Pacific Northwest* [114]. *(University of Washington Libraries, Special Collections, NA891.)*

114. American Indians of the Pacific Northwest

American Memory Project, Library of Congress and University of Washington Libraries
http://memory.loc.gov/ammem/collections/pacific/

These 2,300 photographs and 7,700 pages of text focus on the lives of American Indians in the Northwest Coast and Plateau regions of the Pacific Northwest. Materials illustrate housing, clothing, crafts, transportation, education, employment, and other aspects of everyday life among American Indians in this region. Most of the photographs were taken before 1920. Texts include more than 3,800 pages from the *Annual Reports* of the Commissioner of Indian Affairs to the Secretary of the Interior from 1851 through 1908; eighty-nine *Pacific Northwest Quarterly* articles from 1906 to 1998; and twenty-three titles in the University of Washington *Publications in Anthropology* series. The website also offers fourteen maps and ten lengthy essays authored by anthropologists on specific tribal groups and cross-cultural topics.

115. American Variety Stage: Vaudeville and Popular Entertainment, 1870–1920

American Memory Project, Library of Congress
http://memory.loc.gov/ammem/vshtml/vshome.html

This collection documents the development of vaudeville and other popular entertainment forms from the 1870s to 1920. Materials include 334 English and Yiddish play scripts and 146 theater programs and playbills. Sixty-one motion pictures range from animal acts to dance to dramatic sketches. Ten sound recordings feature comic skits, popular music, and a dramatic monologue. The website also features 143 photos and twenty-nine memorabilia items documenting the life and career of magician Harry Houdini and an essay with links to specific items entitled "Houdini: A Biographical Chronology." Search by keyword or browse the subject and author indexes. The website is linked to the Library of Congress Exhibition "Bob Hope and American Variety," http://www.loc.gov/exhibits/bobhope/, which charts the persistence of a vaudeville tradition in later entertainment forms.

116. Booker T. Washington Papers

University of Illinois Press, History Cooperative
http://www.historycooperative.org/btw/index.html

Booker T. Washington, born a slave in Virginia, became a central figure in the quest for education and equality for African Americans after the Civil War. In 1881, he founded the Tuskegee Normal and Industrial Institute in Alabama and became an influential educator and leader. Washington promoted vocational education for African Americans and was criticized for cultivating white approval. The complete fourteen-volume set of Washington's papers is available on this website, including the well-known "Atlanta Compromise Address" and his autobiography *Up From Slavery*. Texts include books, articles, speeches, and correspondence covering the years 1860 to 1915, and can be searched by keyword. The website also includes hundreds of photographs and illustrations collected in six volumes that accompany the texts.

117. California as I Saw It: First-Person Narratives of California's Early Years, 1849–1900

American Memory Project, Library of Congress
http://memory.loc.gov/ammem/cbhtml/cbhome.html

The 190 works presented on this website—approximately 40,000 written pages and more than 3,000 illustrations—provide eyewitness accounts covering California history from the Gold Rush through the end of the nineteenth century. Most authors represented are white, educated, male Americans, including reporters detailing Gold Rush incidents and visitors from the 1880s attracted to a highly publicized romantic vision of California life. The narratives, in the form of diaries, descriptions, guidebooks, and subsequent reminiscences, portray encounters with those living in California as well as the impact of mining, ranching, and agriculture. Additional topics include urban development, the growth of cities, and California's unique place in American culture. A special presentation recounts early California history, and a discussion of the collection's strengths and weaknesses provides useful context for the first-person accounts.

118. Centennial Exhibition, Philadelphia 1876

Free Library of Philadelphia
http://libwww.library.phila.gov/CenCol/index.htm

The International Exhibition of Arts, Manufactures, and Products of the Soil and Mine, unofficially known as the Centennial Exhibition, was held in Philadelphia in 1876 and was attended by more than nine million people. This website presents 1,500 images, including photographs, lithographs, engravings, maps, scrapbooks, and albums, searchable by keyword or subject, on this event. "Exhibition Facts" provides statistics, a summary of the fair's significance, photographs of buildings erected by foreign nations, and images of sheet music. A timeline traces the fair's lifespan from the 1871 Act of Congress that created its planning commission to the removal of exhibits in December 1876. A bibliography lists more than 130 related works and seventeen websites. "Tours" features an interactive map of the fairgrounds. "Centennial Schoolhouse" offers activities, including excerpts from a seventeen-year-old boy's diary. This website provides revealing images of the event that introduced America "as a new industrial world power."

119. Chicago Anarchists on Trial: Evidence from the Haymarket Affair, 1886–1887

American Memory Project, Library of Congress and Chicago Historical Society

http://memory.loc.gov/ammem/award98/ichihtml/hayhome.html

This collection of documents—roughly 3,800 pages of court proceedings—concerns the Haymarket Affair, a watershed event in the history of American radicalism that led to the first "Red Scare" in America. Materials include autobiographies of two of the eight anarchists tried for conspiracy in the murder of seven Chicago police officers. The officers died after a bomb exploded at an anarchist meeting in May 1886, the day after two workers died in a struggle between police and locked-out union members at the McCormick reaper factory. Four defendants were executed, despite lack of evidence connecting them to the bombing. The website presents approximately 221 newspaper clippings, fifty-five photographs, nineteen letters, nine broadsides, and more than twenty artifacts. A linked exhibition, "The Dramas of Haymarket," furnishes a historical narrative and contextual interpretation. This website is valuable for the study of late nineteenth-century American radicalism, law enforcement, and political climate.

120. The Chinese in California, 1850–1925

American Memory Project, Library of Congress; University of California, Berkeley; and California Historical Society

http://lcweb2.loc.gov/ammem/award99/cubhtml/cichome.html

These 8,000 items document the experiences of Chinese immigrants who settled in California during the nineteenth and early twentieth centuries. Materials include photographs, letters, diaries, speeches, business records, legal documents, pamphlets, sheet music, cartoons, and artwork. Access is provided through nine galleries, each containing an introductory essay and between seventy and 575 items. Four galleries present materials on San Francisco's Chinatown, including architectural space, business and politics, community life, and appeal to outsiders. Additional galleries deal with Chinese involvement in U.S. expansion westward; communities outside San Francisco; agricultural, fishing, and related industries; the anti-Chinese movement and Chinese exclusion; and sentiments concerning the Chinese. Visitors may search by keyword, name, subject, title, group, and theme. The website will be useful for studying ethnic history, labor history, and the history of the West as well as Chinese American history.

Screenshot from *The Chinese in California, 1850–1925* [120]. *(Courtesy of Library of Congress, Prints & Photographs Division.)*

121. David Rumsey Historical Map Collection

David Rumsey, Cartography Associates

http://www.davidrumsey.com/

This private collection presents more than 15,800 rare historical maps with a focus on North and South America. The collection is accessible via several formats. A standard browser (the "directory") is designed for use by the general public. In addition to two browsers and a "collections ticker" requiring Insight software (available for free download), a GIS browser shows detailed overlays of maps and geospatial data for the more serious researcher. Many of the U.S. maps are from the late nineteenth and early twentieth centuries and are often notable for their craftsmanship.

Map, United States of America, G.W. Colton, 1856, from the *David Rumsey Historical Map Collection* [121]. *(Courtesy of the David Rumsey Map Collection, www.davidrumsey.com.)*

Materials include atlases, globes, books, maritime charts, pocket and wall maps, and children's maps. Users can zoom in to view details. Overlay capabilities make this website valuable for its ability to convey how locations have changed over time.

122. Emergence of Advertising in America: 1850–1920

John W. Hartman Center and Duke University Digital Scriptorium
http://library.duke.edu/digitalcollections/eaa/

Advertisement, Eastman Kodak Brownie Camera, 1900, from *Emergence of Advertising in America: 1850–1920* [122]. *(Hartman Center for Sales, Advertising and Marketing History of the Rare Book, Manuscript & Special Collections Library, Duke University.)*

These 9,000 advertising items and publications date from 1850 to 1920. Selected items illustrate the rise of consumer culture in America and the development of a professionalized advertising industry. Images are grouped into eleven categories: advertising ephemera (trade cards, calendars, almanacs, postcards); broadsides for placement on walls, fences, and buildings; advertising cookbooks from food companies and appliance manufacturers; early advertising agency publications created to promote the concepts and methods of the industry; promotional literature from the nation's oldest advertising agency, J. Walter Thompson; early Kodak print advertisements; Lever Brothers Lux (soap) advertisements; R.C. Maxwell advertising company images; outdoor advertising; scrapbooks; and tobacco ads. Each category contains a brief overview, and each image is accompanied by production information. The website, searchable by keyword or ad content, includes a timeline on the history of advertising from the 1850s to 1920. This easy-to-use collection is ideal for researching consumer culture and marketing strategies.

123. Evolution of the Conservation Movement, 1850–1920

American Memory Project, Library of Congress
http://lcweb2.loc.gov/ammem/amrvhtml/conshome.html

These published works, manuscripts, images, and motion picture footage address the formation of the movement to conserve and protect America's natural heritage. Materials include sixty-two books and pamphlets, 140 federal statutes and congressional resolutions, thirty-four additional legislative documents, and excerpts from the *Congressional Globe* and the *Congressional Record*. An additional 360 presidential proclamations, 170 prints and photographs, two historic manuscripts, and two motion pictures are available. Materials include Alfred Bierstadt paintings, period travel literature, a photographic record of Yosemite, and congressional acts regarding conservation and the establishment of national parks. An annotated chronology discusses events in the development of the conservation movement with links to pertinent documents and images.

124. Great Chicago Fire and the Web of Memory

Chicago Historical Society and Northwestern University
http://www.chicagohs.org/fire/index.html

This exhibit commemorates the 125th anniversary of the Great Chicago Fire (1871) with an array of primary sources arranged into two sections. "The Great Chicago Fire" examines the fire through five chronological chapters, while a second section, "The Web of Memory," focuses on the ways in which the fire has been remembered. This section presents the story through eyewitness accounts, popular illustrations, journal articles, fiction, poetry, and painting. It also examines the legend of Mrs. O'Leary. The website furnishes galleries of images and artifacts, primary texts, songs, a newsreel, an "Interactive Panorama of Chicago, 1858," and background essays that explore the social and cultural context of the fire and its aftermath.

125. HarpWeek: Explore History

John Adler

http://www.harpweek.com/

Some resources available on this website are free while others require a subscription. Twenty-two exhibits present free access to a wealth of texts and images on a variety of subjects dealing with nineteenth-century American history. Each section provides illustrations, articles, editorials, and overviews. Materials include four

Cover of *Harper's Weekly* depicting "The Herald of Relief from America," from *HarpWeek: Explore History* [125]. *(Provided courtesy of HarpWeek, LLC.)*

exhibits on politics and elections, including the impeachment of Andrew Johnson. Six exhibits deal with race and ethnicity, including slavery and Chinese Americans. Three exhibits offer material on business and consumer culture, such as advertising history and tobacco. Additional exhibits include "The American West," "A Sampler of Civil War Literature," "Russian-American Relations, 1863–1905," and "The World of Thomas Nast." A subscription-based website presents the entire run of *Harper's Weekly*, **http://www.alexanderstreet.com/products/harp.htm**. With free registration, *Nineteenth-Century Advertising*, **http://advertising.harpweek.com**, presents an archive of 40,000 advertisements that appeared in *Harper's Weekly*.

126. Indian Peoples of the Northern Great Plains

Institute of Museum and Library Services
http://www.lib.montana.edu/epubs/nadb/

These 685 items represent twenty-seven current and former Native American tribes of the Northern Great Plains and cover a period from 1870 to 1954. Most of the materials are photographs with identifying text. The collection also includes stereographs, ledger drawings, and other sketches. Users can view three unique collections. The "Barstow Ledger Drawing Collection" offers sixty-six Crow and Gros Ventre drawings from the late nineteenth century. A portfolio entitled "Blackfeet Indian Tipis, Design and Legend" includes twenty-six works and an introductory essay. Another collection offers treaties with the Assiniboine, Blackfeet, and North Piegan tribes from 1874 and 1875. Searching is available by subject, date, location, name, tribe, collection, and artist or photographer. This valuable website documents folkways, material culture, and the history of Native Americans from the Northern Great Plains region.

127. Kate and Sue McBeth, Missionary Teachers to the Nez Perce Indians

Rose Huskey, Donna K. Smith, and Bill Kerr, University of Idaho
http://www.lib.uidaho.edu/mcbeth/index.htm

Presenting full-text letters and diaries, this website focuses on the lives and careers of Kate and Sue McBeth, missionaries and teachers among the Nez Perce Indians during the last quarter of the nineteenth century. Government documents and images pertaining to the tribe's history accompany these materials. Sue McBeth established a successful theological seminary for Nez Perce men, collected and organized a Nez Perce/English dictionary, and wrote journal articles. Kate McBeth provided literacy education for Nez Perce women, taught Euro-American domestic skills, and directed a Sabbath school and mission society. Divided into five sections, materials include more than 150 letters, a diary, a journal, five treaties, more than seventy commission and agency reports and legislative actions, excerpts from a history of the Nez Perce, and nineteen biographies. Six maps and approximately one hundred images, including thirteen illustrations depicting the 1855 Walla Walla Treaty negotiations, are also available.

128. Making of America

University of Michigan
http://quod.lib.umich.edu/m/moagrp/

Making of America

Cornell University
http://cdl.library.cornell.edu/moa/

Together, these two websites provide more than 1.5 million pages of text in a collaborative effort to digitize more than 11,000 volumes and 100,000 journal articles from the nineteenth century. The websites present full-text access to thirty-two journals, including literary and political magazines such as *Atlantic Monthly* and *Harper's New Monthly Magazine*. The list includes specialized journals as well, such as *Scientific American, Manufacturer and Builder, Ladies Repository*, and the *American Missionary*. The websites also offer an abundance of novels and monographs. A recent addition provides 249 volumes on New York City, some from the early twentieth century. At present, the two collections remain separate and must be searched individually. The institutions plan to integrate their websites, however, and to include material from other major research libraries. Access to many *Making of America* texts is also available through the Library of Congress's American Memory Project website, *The Nineteenth Century in Print* (**http://memory.loc.gov/ammem/ndlpcoop/moahtml/ncphome.html**).

129. Mark Twain in His Times

Stephen Railton, University of Virginia
http://etext.lib.virginia.edu/railton/

Based on Mark Twain's works and life, this engaging website focuses on the creation of the author's popular image, the marketing and promotion of his texts, and live performances. Five sections center on major works, including *Innocents Abroad, Tom Sawyer*, and *Pudd'nhead Wilson*. Each section is placed in historical context. The website offers an extensive collection of text sources, including fifty published texts or lectures, sixteen letters, and more than one hundred texts and excerpts from other late nineteenth-century authors. Twenty-nine items from publishers, more than eighty newspaper and magazine articles, thirty-five obituary notices, more than one hundred period literary reviews, and hundreds of illustrations and photographs round out this informative website. An interactive graphic essay explores the issue of racism through various American illustrations of "Jim" in *Huckleberry Finn*. This is an invaluable resource for studying American literature and its place within the nineteenth-century marketplace and landscape.

130. Native American Documents Project

E. A. Schwartz, California State University at San Marcos
http://www2.csusm.edu/nadp/nadp.htm

These four collections of data and documents address federal Indian policy in the late nineteenth century. The first set includes eight annual reports of the

Commissioner of Indian Affairs from the 1870s, along with appendices and a map. The second set, "Allotment Data," traces the federal "reform" policy of dividing Indian lands into small tracts for individuals—a significant amount of which went to whites—from the 1870s to the 1910s. This set includes transcriptions of five acts of Congress, tables, and an essay analyzing the data. The third set includes 111 documents on the little-known Rogue River War of 1855 in Oregon, the reservations set up for Indian survivors, and the allotment of one of these reservations, the Siletz, in 1894. The fourth set provides the California section of an ethnographic compilation from 1952.

131. Nineteenth-Century California Sheet Music

Mary Kay Duggan, Museum Informatics Project, University of California, Berkeley
http://people.ischool.berkeley.edu/~mkduggan/neh.html

These scanned images come from more than 2,700 pieces of sheet music published between 1852 and 1900 in California. The website also includes more than 800 illustrated covers, forty-eight audio selections, eight video clips of singers, and a handful of programs, posters, playbills, periodicals, catalogs, broadsheets, books on music, and maps. More than 350 items contain advertising. Explanatory essays of 1,000 to 2,000 words provide general information on music from more than a dozen ethnic cultures, and include references to specific topics, including buildings, composers, dance, disasters, gender, mining, performers, politics, product ads, railroads, and sports. The website also provides fourteen links to additional sheet music collections and reference sources. These resources are valuable for studying popular culture, California history, music history, advertising, and depictions of ethnicity, gender, and race in nineteenth-century America.

132. Prairie Settlement: Nebraska Photographs
and Family Letters

American Memory Project, Library of Congress and Nebraska State Historical Society
http://memory.loc.gov/ammem/award98/nbhihtml/

These two collections illuminate life on the Great Plains from 1862 to 1912. The nearly 3,500 glass plate negatives depict everyday life in central Nebraska, with images of businesses, farms, people, churches, and fairs in four counties. Approximately 318 letters describe the sojourn of the Uriah Oblinger family through Indiana, Nebraska, Minnesota, Kansas, and Missouri as they traveled to establish a homestead. Letters discuss such topics as land, work, neighbors, crops, religious meetings, grasshoppers, financial troubles, and Nebraska's Easter Blizzard of 1873. A 1,000-word essay describes the letter collection and the lives of the principal correspondents. Biographical notes are available for more than 120 of the people who corresponded with the Oblingers or who were mentioned in the letters.

133. Sanborn Fire Insurance Maps, Utah

J. Willard Marriott Library, University of Utah
http://www.lib.utah.edu/digital/collections/sanborn/

These 1,275 detailed historical maps depict cities in the state of Utah. D. A. Sanborn Company, a pioneer producer of insurance maps on a national scale, designed maps that depicted commercial, industrial, and residential sections of Utah cities. The collection of large-scale detailed maps dating from 1867 through 1969 is an ongoing project, and currently contains maps of forty cities. Users may download compressed images to view and enhance the maps. Maps are arranged alphabetically by city and date, although the years available for each city are inconsistent. The maps outline the site, size, shape, construction, and building materials of dwellings, commercial buildings, and factories. In addition, the maps detail building use, sidewalks, property boundaries, house and block numbers, and even the location of hydrants and wells. The collection presents an opportunity to study Utah history, architectural history, and the development of cartography.

134. Small-Town America: Stereoscopic Views from the Robert Dennis Collection, 1850–1920

American Memory Project, Library of Congress and New York Public Library
http://memory.loc.gov/ammem/award97/nyplhtml/dennhome.html

More than 12,000 stereoscopic photographs depict life in small towns, villages, rural areas, and cities throughout New York, New Jersey, and Connecticut from 1850 to 1920. Materials include pictures of buildings, street scenes, natural landscapes, agriculture, industry, transportation, homes, businesses, local celebrations, natural disasters, and people. Each grouping of photographs offers a short description of the contents as well as notes on the locations, medium, collection names, and digital identification information. The website also features an essay on the history of stereoscopic views and nine related website links. The website is searchable by keyword and can be browsed by subject and image name. These revealing illustrations are valuable for examining rural and urban development as well as everyday life.

135. Taking the Long View: Panoramic Photographs, 1851–1991

American Memory Project, Library of Congress
http://memory.loc.gov/ammem/collections/panoramic_photo/

Nearly 4,000 panoramic photographs of cityscapes, landscapes, and group portraits, deposited as copyright submissions by more than 400 companies, are displayed on this website. Panoramic photographs were used to advertise real estate and to document groups, events, and gatherings. Images depict all fifty states, the District of Columbia, and more than twenty foreign countries and territories. Subjects include cityscapes, landscapes, group portraits, agricultural life, disasters, education, engineering, fairs and expositions, industrial scenes, military activities, performing arts, sports, and transportation. Although the images cover the period from 1851 to 1991, the collection centers on the early twentieth century. The website includes a bibliography, an illustrated 1,000-word background essay on the history of panoramic photography, and an essay outlining the technicality of shooting a panoramic photograph. Four essays focus on specific photographers: George R. Lawrence (1869–1938), George N. Barnard (1819–1902), Frederick W. Brehm (1871–1950), and Miles F. Weaver (1879–1932).

136. Thomas A. Edison Papers

Rutgers State University of New Jersey; National Park Service; New Jersey Historical Commission; Smithsonian Institution

http://edison.rutgers.edu/

A vast database of Thomas Edison's papers, this website includes 71,000 pages of correspondence, 12,000 pages of technical drawings, and more than 13,000 clippings about the inventor from 103 journals and newspapers. In total, the website boasts more than five million pages of documents related to Edison. Processes for searching the website are complicated, but an extensive guide offers search strategies. Materials include 2,210 facsimiles of Edison patents from 1868 to 1931 for products such as the electric lamp and the phonograph. A collection of fourteen photographs, maps, and prints depict Edison, his environs, and his inventions. The website offers a "Document Sampler" of twenty-three selections of general interest as well as an 8,000-word essay on Edison's companies, twenty-two pages about Edison and the development of the motion picture industry, and two chronologies. A bibliography directs visitors to more than seventy books and articles and twenty-one related websites.

137. Votes for Women: Selections from the National American Woman Suffrage Association Collection, 1848–1921

American Memory Project, Library of Congress

http://memory.loc.gov/ammem/naw/nawshome.html

Covering the years from 1848 to 1921, this website presents materials from the suffrage movement in America, including 167 books, pamphlets, handbooks, reports, speeches, and other artifacts totaling some 10,000 pages. Formed in 1890 from two rival groups, the National American Woman Suffrage Association (NAWSA) orchestrated passage of the Nineteenth Amendment in 1920 through state campaigns. Materials include works by Carrie Chapman Catt, the association's longtime president, as well as from other officers and members, including Elizabeth Cady Stanton, Susan B. Anthony, Lucy Stone, Alice Stone Blackwell, Julia Ward Howe, Elizabeth Smith Miller, and Mary A. Livermore. There are two bibliographies, an essay on Catt, a timeline, and links to eighteen related collections, most of them associated with the Library of Congress's American Memory Project.

Emergence of Modern America, 1890–1930

138. Alcohol, Temperance, and Prohibition

Brown University Library

http://dl.lib.brown.edu/temperance/

This small, but useful, website offers a wide range of primary source material for researching the history of the prohibition movement, temperance, and alcoholism. The more than 1,800 items include broadsides, sheet music, pamphlets, and government publications related to the temperance movement and prohibition. Materials come from the period leading up to prohibition, such as an 1830s broadside on the

"Absent Father" as well as the prohibition era itself, such as a 1920 pamphlet entitled "Alcohol Sides with Germ Enemies." They end with the passage of the Twenty-First Amendment, which repealed prohibition in 1933. All digitized items are in the public domain. An essay, "Temperance and Prohibition Era Propaganda: A Study in Rhetoric" by Leah Rae Berk, provides an overview of the topic and historical context.

139. Amateur Athletic Foundation Digital Archive

Amateur Athletic Foundation of Los Angeles
http://www.la84foundation.org/5va/over_frmst.htm

For those studying the history of the Olympics, sports history, and the history of leisure and recreation, this website provides more than 45,000 documents (in PDF format) pertaining to official Olympics history, as well as other sports. Complete or partial runs of ten journals have been digitized, including *Journal of Sports History* (3,030 articles from 1974 to 2003), *Olympic Review* (1901–2003), *Baseball Magazine* (1909–1918), *American Golfer* (1908–1911), *Golf Illustrated and Outdoor Man* (1914–1915), and *Outing* (1883–1899). The website also furnishes fifty-eight oral histories of Southern California Olympic athletes and eighty-three official Olympic Reports from 1896 to 2004. The full text of *This Great Symbol: Pierre de Coubertin and the Origins of the Modern Olympic Games* by John MacAloon and some recent studies of aspects of sports history are also available. Additions to the website are made regularly.

140. America at Work, America at Leisure: Motion Pictures from 1894–1915

American Memory Project, Library of Congress
http://memory.loc.gov/ammem/awlhtml/awlhome.html

This collection of 150 motion pictures produced between 1894 and 1915 deals with work, school, and leisure activities in the United States. The films include footage of the U.S. Postal Service in 1903, cattle breeding, fire fighters, ice manufacturing, logging, physical education classes, amusement parks, sporting events, and local festivals and parades. Each film is accompanied by a brief summary. A special presentation furnishes additional information on three categories: America at school, work, and leisure. Essays of roughly 1,000 words provide context and general descriptions of films in each category, display fifteen illustrative photographs, and link to related films. A thirty-one-work bibliography provides suggestions for further reading and websites on American labor, education, and leisure.

141. American Environmental Photographs, 1891–1936

American Memory Project, Library of Congress
http://memory.loc.gov/ammem/collections/ecology/index.html

These approximately 4,500 photographs document natural environments, ecologies, and plant communities in the United States at the end of the nineteenth and the beginning of the twentieth centuries. Produced by American botanists between 1891 and 1936, the photos describe various ecosystems and landforms across the United States. Users can search for specific plants and some animals as well as for landforms, natural events, and weather patterns. The collection is a bit odd in that it mixes genres and types. Clicking on the region "Pennsylvania" produces eight images, ranging from pictures of dogwoods to a photo of tree rings to three pictures of the Pittsburgh flood. A timeline and an essay on "Ecology and the American Environment" provide valuable background information as well as a bibliography. These materials are useful as a record of early environmental thinking as well as a document of vanished landscapes.

142. American Family Immigration History Center

The Statue of Liberty-Ellis Island Foundation Inc.
http://www.ellisisland.org/

Records on the more than twenty-five million passengers and ship crew members who passed through Ellis Island between 1892 and 1924 are available through this website. Most passengers came from Europe and Russia, although there are some records from Asia, the Caribbean, and Latin America. The website requires a free, simple registration to view detailed records that include name, residence, date of arrival, age on arrival, ethnicity, place of residence, marital status, ship of travel, place of departure, and a copy of the original ship manifest (a transcription is also available). The website includes extensive contextual information about Ellis Island, immigration, and genealogical research. "Family Histories" illuminates the genealogical research experiences of six Americans of diverse ethnic backgrounds. The "Peopling of America" exhibit covers six periods from pre-1790 to 2000, with graphs, photographs, and immigration statistics geared to place of origin. Additional information is available for an annual fee.

143. American Leaders Speak: Recordings from World War I and the 1920 Election

American Memory Project, Library of Congress
http://memory.loc.gov/ammem/nfhtml/

These fifty-nine sound recordings document speeches by American leaders produced from 1918 to 1920 on the Nation's Forum record label. The speeches—by such prominent public figures as Warren G. Harding, James M. Cox, Calvin Coolidge, Franklin D. Roosevelt, Samuel Gompers, Henry Cabot Lodge, John J. Pershing, Will H. Hays, A. Mitchell Palmer, and Rabbi Stephen S. Wise—deal for the most part with issues and events related to World War I and the 1920 presidential election. Additional topics include social unrest, Americanism, bolshevism, taxes, and business practices. Speeches range from one to five minutes in length. A special presentation, "From War to Normalcy," introduces the collection with representative recordings, including Harding's famous pronouncement that Americans need "not nostrums but normalcy." This website includes photographs of speakers and of the actual recording disk labels, as well as text versions of the speeches.

144. American Radicalism Collection

Special Collections and Digital Sources Center, Michigan State University Libraries
http://www.lib.msu.edu/coll/main/spec_col/radicalism/index.htm

This website contains 129 pamphlets, documents, and newsletters produced by or relevant to radical movements. Groups represented by one to thirty documents include the American Indian Movement, Asian Americans, the Black Panthers, the Hollywood Ten, the Ku Klux Klan, the IWW, and the Students for a Democratic Society. Additional situations covered include the Rosenberg case, Sacco and Vanzetti, and the Scottsboro Boys. Additional topics include birth control and the events at Wounded Knee. This is a small but useful resource on radicalism, political movements, and rhetoric.

145. Anti-Saloon League, 1893–1933

Beth Weinhardt, Westerville, Ohio Public Library
http://www.wpl.lib.oh.us:80/AntiSaloon/

These printed materials are representative of the public campaigns of the Anti-Saloon League from 1893 to 1933. A six-page history of the League and the temperance movement and six biographical essays of movement leaders provide context. Facsimiles of eighty-nine fliers produced by the League advocate temperance with arguments that include the effect of alcohol on puppies and German Emperor William II's opinion of drinking. A periodical section reproduces three covers, three sample articles, and one complete 1912 issue of *American Patriot*, a temperance magazine, and one cover of *American Issue*. Other material includes fourteen wet and dry maps of the United States produced by the League, three temperance anthems, transcriptions of nine anti-alcohol stories, and twelve pro-temperance cartoons. In addition, six entries from the *Standard Encyclopedia of the Alcohol Problem*, published between 1925 and 1930, offer the Temperance perspective on communion wine, whiskey production, and alcohol use in China.

146. Around the World in the 1890s: Photographs from
the World's Transportation Commission, 1894–1896

American Memory Project, Library of Congress
http://memory.loc.gov/ammem/wtc/wtchome.html

More than 900 photographs taken by American photographer William Henry Jackson (1843–1942) during his tour of North Africa, Asia, Russia, Australia, and Oceania from 1894 to 1896 are presented here. The World's Transportation Commission, an organization formed to aid American business interests abroad, commissioned Jackson for this trip. The photographs, originally exhibited in Chicago's Field Columbian Museum, focus on transportation systems, especially railroads, as well as tourist sites, indigenous life, wildlife, and locations of natural beauty. Nearly 687 of the images are from lantern slides, many of which were hand-colored. Many of the photographs appeared in *Harper's Weekly*. This collection is valuable for those interested in late nineteenth-century photography, colonialism, and industrialization.

147. Child Labor in America, 1908–1912:
Photographs of Lewis W. Hine

The History Place
http://www.historyplace.com/unitedstates/childlabor/index.html

These sixty-four photographs taken by Lewis W. Hine (1874–1940) between 1908 and 1912 document American children working in mills, mines, streets, and factories,

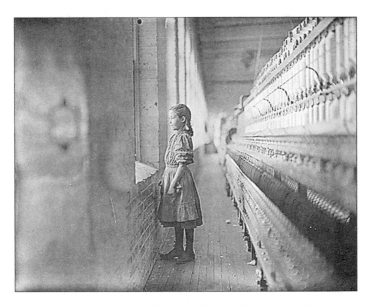

Photograph, eleven-year-old mill worker, Rhodes Manufacturing Company, Lincolnton, NC, from *Child Labor in America, 1908–1912: Photographs of Lewis W. Hine* [147]. *(Courtesy The History Place [www.historyplace.com].)*

and as "newsies," seafood workers, fruit pickers, and salesmen. The website also includes photographs of immigrant families and children's "pastimes and vices." Original captions by Hine — one of the most influential photographers in American history — call attention to exploitative and unhealthy conditions for laboring children. A background essay introduces Hine and the history of child labor in the United States. This is a valuable collection for studying documentary photography, urban history, labor history, and the social history of the Progressive era.

148. Clash of Cultures in the 1910s and 1920s

Matthew Davis and Pamela Pennock, Ohio State University
http://ehistory.osu.edu/osu/mmh/clash/default.htm

This 10,000-word interpretive essay on the culture wars of the 1910s and 1920s is organized into four sections. It offers thirty-four documents and seventy-five images — photographs, cartoons, posters, flyers, and maps — to provide historical context and connections between seemingly unrelated phenomena. "Prohibition" includes an exhibition of photographs, political cartoons, and documents from the Ohio Dry Campaign of 1918. "Anti-Immigration and the KKK" presents a Klansman's manual, anti-immigration magazine articles, and the text of the Immigration Act of 1924. "The New Woman" contains sections on image and lifestyle, sexuality, opposition, the African American New Woman, and work, education, and reform. "The Scopes Trial" includes documents on fundamentalism and evolution and trial transcripts. The website provides twenty-eight related links and bibliographies of forty-two titles. This valuable website emphasizes the complexity of conflicts persistent throughout twentieth-century American history.

149. Cylinder Preservation and Digitization Project

UC Santa Barbara, Department of Special Collections
http://cylinders.library.ucsb.edu/

Cylinder recordings were the first commercially produced sound recordings. This extensive collection of more than 6,000 cylinder recordings from the late nineteenth and early twentieth centuries (1890 to 1928) allows visitors to explore this era of sound recording that is often overlooked in the study of American musical history. Users can browse the collection by performer, title, label, or year of release or they can search the collection by keyword, author, title, subject, or year. Recordings stream online and are available for download. The project overview describes the technical issues involved in the project, explains variations in recording quality, and provides a warning about the potentially offensive "dialect recordings" and why they were included. There are also links to thirty-six related websites.

150. Digital Archive Collections at the University of Hawai'i at Manoa Library

University of Hawai'i System Libraries
http://library.manoa.hawaii.edu/research/digicoll.html

These twenty-nine collections document the history of Hawaii and Micronesia from 1834 to the 1990s. "Annexation of Hawai'i," for example, contains thousands of pages of documents concerning the U.S. plan to annex Hawaii, realized in 1898. Materials include the 1,437-page *Blount Report* of 1894–1895, initiated by President Grover Cleveland, on the history of relations between the United States and Hawaii and the planned annexation; congressional debates on the Hawaii Organic Act, passed in 1900 to establish a territorial government; and Hawaiian anti-annexation petitions and protest documents from 1897 to 1898. "Hawaii War Records" presents 880 photographs documenting the impact of World War II on Hawaii and its people. "Trust Territories of the Pacific Islands" photo archive provides 52,000 photographs on programs in education, health, political, and economic development in the 2,100 islands of Micronesia administered by the United States from 1947 to 1994. The website also includes a collection of sixteen Hawaiian language newspapers.

151. Dime Novels and Penny Dreadfuls

Stanford University
http://www-sul.stanford.edu/depts/dp/pennies/home.html

More than 2,300 covers of American "dime novels," and their British counterparts, the "penny dreadfuls," are available on this website. In addition, the full-text of nine books and a series entitled *Secret Service* (1899–1912) are available. The website offers "guided tours" with images and essays of approximately 1,500 words on print processes and dime novel covers. The full-text selections include stories featuring such heroes as Nick Carter, Buffalo Bill, Jesse James, Deadwood Dick, Fred Fearnot, and Calamity Jane. A full-text search is available only for those users affiliated with Stanford University. The website provides basic information on each title and indexes books according to subject, genre, setting, intended audience age and gender, and type of graphic material. Subject indexing of cover iconography is especially valuable. Listings are organized according to depictions of ethnicity/nationality,

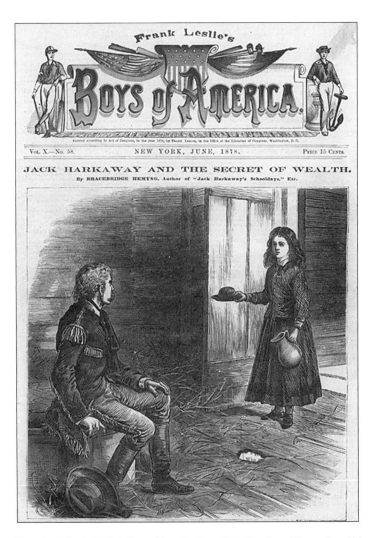

Page from Frank Leslie's *Boys of America* from *Dime Novels and Penny Dreadfuls* [151]. *(Courtesy of Department of Special Collections, Stanford University Libraries.)*

occupation, types of places, types of sports and recreations, types of violence, and types of gestures and actions classified according to gender of character portrayed.

152. Edward S. Curtis's *The North American Indian*

American Memory Project, Library of Congress and Northwestern University Library
http://lcweb2.loc.gov/ammem/award98/ienhtml/curthome.html

More than 2,000 photographs, taken by Edward S. Curtis for his work *The North American Indian*, are presented here. These striking images of North American tribes are considered some of the most significant representations produced during a time of rapid change. They can be browsed by subjects such as persons, custom, jewelry, tools, and buildings. Each image is accompanied by comprehensive iden-

Photograph, Luzi-Papago, 1908, from *Edward S. Curtis's* The
North American Indian [152]. *(McCormick Library of Special
Collections, Northwestern University Library.)*

tifying data and Curtis's original captions. The voluminous collection and narrative
are presented in twenty volumes. Photographs can be browsed by subject, eighty
American Indian tribe names, and seven geographic locations. This website also
features a twelve-item bibliography and three scholarly essays discussing Curtis's
methodology as an ethnographer, the significance of his work to native peoples
of North America, and his promotion of the twentieth-century view that Native
Americans were a "vanishing race." The biographical timeline and map depicting
locations where Curtis photographed indigenous groups are especially useful.

153. 1896: The Presidential Campaign

Rebecca Edwards and Sarah DeFeo, Vassar College
http://projects.vassar.edu/1896/1896home.html

The election of 1896 was one of the most contentious in U.S. history. When Republican William McKinley defeated William Jennings Bryan on November third, there

Cartoon from the *Judge*, 25 July 1896, from *1896: The Presidential Campaign* [153]. *(Cartoon courtesy of the Presidential Campaign: Cartoons and Commentary, http://projects.vassar.edu/1896/1896home.html.)*

were no fewer than six candidates on the ballot and the country was in the throes of an economic depression. This website provides close to one hundred political cartoons surrounding the election campaigns. The website acts like a virtual web of knowledge, with linked words in almost every sentence leading to helpful chunks of information on key themes, political parties and their leaders, print culture, and popular culture. Together, this information sheds light not only on the political situation in the 1890s, but also on the social, economic, and cultural contexts of the era. Special sections are devoted to, among many other topics, the bicycle craze, anti-Semitism, popular amusements, the Supreme Court, and women's suffrage. An extensive bibliography and a section devoted to teaching suggestions are also included.

154. Emma Goldman Papers

Berkeley Digital Library
http://sunsite.berkeley.edu/Goldman/

Emma Goldman (1869–1940) was a major figure in the radical and feminist movements in the United States prior to her deportation in 1919. This collection of primary resources includes selections from four books by Goldman, as well as eighteen published essays and pamphlets, four speeches, forty-nine letters, and five newspaper accounts of Goldman's activities. There are also nearly forty photographs, illustrations, and facsimiles of documents. Additional items include two biographical exhibitions, selections from a published guide of documentary sources, and four sample documents from the book edition of her papers. A curriculum for students is designed to aid the study of freedom of expression, women's rights, anti-militarism, and social change. The website offers essays on the project's history, as well as bibliographic references and links to other websites.

ST. TROPEZ 29 April 1 9 2 9

Dear Theodore:

I have just had a letter from my friend Eleanor Fitzgerald about a talk she has had with you. She seems to be under the impression that you were a bit put out because I did not send you more material for your forthcoming portrait of me. Now really, old man, you should not feel hurt. I am surprised that you dont know how much I appreciate what you want to do for me. If I have seemed ungracious I hope you will forgive me. There certainly was no intention on my part of being that.

Being a writer you should know how difficult it is to tear anything out of a book, even if I could take the time now in the midst of my writing. I dont know, anyway, what it is t hat you want. For instance, Fitzi tells me that you want something of my background. What particular part of it? You see, I have written chapters and chapters on my home, my family, my childhood, and all the other things of my youth. They are so much a part of the rest of the story that I hardly see how they can be detached from their context. Nevertheless I will make an attempt to send something to you, provided you tell me exactly what it is you want. Please write me soon and give me an idea of how I can help you.

Believe me, it is not an exaggeration when I say that the least little thing which takes me away from the book or the thoughts I have been living through in the past puts me out for several days, so that I go on again with the greatest effort. Perhaps it is because I am not a ready writer. I find it excruciating to keep at my book, yet I have kept at it for ten months--and it will be many more before even the first draft is finished. I am telling you this so you can know it wasnt lack of appreciation on my part if I did not respond in the way you wanted me to do. Please let me hear from you again soon, and I will see what I can do.

Cordially yours,

E Goldman
Emma

Letter from Emma Goldman to Theodore Dreiser, 29 April 1929, from *Emma Goldman Papers* [154]. *(Theodore Dreiser Papers, Rare Book & Manuscript Library, University of Pennsylvania.)*

155. Eugenics Archive

DNA Learning Center, Cold Spring Harbor Laboratory
http://www.eugenicsarchive.org/eugenics/

The history of the eugenics movement in the United States, from its inception in the decades following the Civil War through its height in the first few decades of the twentieth century, is traced on this website. As we move into the age of genetics, this movement, that sought to filter "bad" traits from the human population, becomes increasingly important to understand. The movement's history is told through a narrative divided into eight themes, including social and scientific origins, research methods and traits studied, flaws in these methods, ways in which the movement was popularized, immigration restriction, and marriage and sterilization laws. Each narrative is accompanied by roughly ten primary sources—reports, articles, charts, legal documents, and photographs. These materials provide a succinct introduction to eugenics in the United States, though the website is in Flash and the primary sources are not available for download.

156. First World War: The War to End All Wars

Michael Duffy
http://www.firstworldwar.com/index.htm

The stated purpose of this website is to provide an overview of World War I. This it does effectively through hundreds of essays, 3,100 encyclopedic entries, 618 biographies, 318 resources on the war's major diplomatic and military events, and a timeline. Primary documents include more than one hundred diaries and first-hand accounts of soldiers and politicians, 3,900 photographs, 651 propaganda posters, and 155 audio files of songs and speeches. Documents include treaties, reports, correspondence, memoirs, speeches, dispatches, and accounts of battles and sieges. The website also provides ninety-five essays on literary figures who wrote about the war. While admittedly a work-in-progress, the website offers much material on the leaders who engaged their countries in war and on the experiences of ordinary soldiers who fought the battles.

157. Harlem: Mecca of the New Negro

Matthew Kirschenbaum and Catherine Tousignant, Electronic Text Center, University of Virginia
http://etext.lib.virginia.edu/harlem/index.html

The complete facsimile and transcript versions of the March 1925 *Survey Graphic* special "Harlem Number," edited by Alain Locke, is presented here. Locke later republished and expanded the contents as the famous *New Negro* anthology. The effort constituted "the first of several attempts to formulate a political and cultural representation of the New Negro and the Harlem community" of the 1920s. The journal is divided into three sections: "The Greatest Negro Community in the World," "The Negro Expresses Himself," and "Black and White—Studies in Race Contacts." The website also includes essays by Locke, W. E. B. Du Bois, and James Weldon Johnson; poems by Countee Cullen, Anne Spencer, Angelina Grimke, Claude McKay, Jean Toomer, and Langston Hughes; and quotations from reviews of the issue.

158. History of the American West, 1860–1920

American Memory Project, Library of Congress and Denver Public Library
http://memory.loc.gov/ammem/award97/codhtml/hawphome.html

More than 30,000 photographs of Colorado towns, landscapes, mining scenes, and Native American tribes, taken between 1860 and 1920, are featured on this website. Approximately 4,000 images deal with the mining industry, including labor strikes, while 3,500 photographs depict communities from more than forty indigenous tribes west of the Mississippi River. Special presentations include a gallery of more than forty photographs depicting the dwellings, children, and daily lives of Native American women; more than thirty images of buildings, statues, and parks in Denver built in conformance with the turn-of-the-century "City Beautiful" movement; and twenty World War II–era photographs of the Tenth Mountain Division, ski troops from Colorado who fought in Italy. Each image in these special exhibits is accompanied by a brief description. There are biographies of three western photographers.

159. Inventing Entertainment: The Early Motion
Pictures and Sound Recordings of the
Edison Companies

American Memory Project, Library of Congress
http://lcweb2.loc.gov/ammem/edhtml/edhome.html

These materials—341 early motion pictures from 1891 to 1918, eighty-one sound recordings from 1913 to 1920, and related materials, such as photographs and original magazine articles—document Thomas Edison's impact on the history of American entertainment. Edison's inventions included the phonograph, the kinetograph motion picture camera, and the kinetoscope motion picture viewer. Sound recordings are accessible by title and according to six genres: instrumental selections, popular vocals, spoken word, spoken comedy, foreign language and ethnic recordings, and opera and concert recordings. Films are organized by title, chronologically, and according to genres, including actualities (non-fiction films), advertising, animation, drama and adventure, experimental, humorous, trick, and reenactments. Actuality subjects include disasters, expositions, famous people, foreign places, the navy, police and fire departments, railroads, scenic America, sports and leisure, the variety stage, and war. Special pages focus on the life of the inventor and his contribution to motion picture and sound recording technologies.

160. Jack London's Writings

Berkeley Digital Library SunSITE
http://london.sonoma.edu/Writings/

The full-text versions of more than forty works by Jack London (1876–1916), a prominent early twentieth-century writer who was also involved in the socialist movement, are available here. Materials include famous fiction, such as *The Call of the Wild* (1903), and lesser-known works, such as *War of the Classes* (1905), as well as a collection of speeches London delivered on behalf of socialism. The website includes twenty novels, nineteen short story collections, two collections of essays, three plays, and six additional published non-fiction works. All materials are keyword searchable. There is no biographical or historical information about London and his times, but when used with other contextual materials, this site's content can be valuable for studying early twentieth-century American literature and journalism and its relation to radical political and social currents of the time.

161. Jewish Women's Archive

Gail Twersky Reimer
http://jwa.org/

These exhibits and resources are valuable for studying American Jewish women's contributions to their communities and the wider world. "Women of Valor" focuses on sixteen notable historic women—including Congresswoman Bella Abzug; radical Emma Goldman; philanthropist Rebecca Gratz; poet Emma Lazarus; actress Molly Picon; Hadassah founder Henrietta Szold; and nurse, settlement worker, and political leader Lillian Wald. "Women Who Dared" offers oral history interviews of Jewish women activists in text, audio, and video formats. Interviewees discuss activism in the context of Jewish and gender identity, values, and situations, and elucidate the path to activism, challenges, rewards, and impact. The website has also digitized nine volumes of *The American Jewess*. Most recently, the Jewish Women's Archive has compiled objects, photographs, and personal accounts of the Hurricane Katrina disaster and the aftermath, complete with one hundred oral histories, blog postings, emails, and other first-hand accounts.

162. Like a Family: The Making of a Southern Cotton Mill World

James Leloudis and Kathryn Walbert, University of North Carolina, Chapel Hill
http://www.ibiblio.org/sohp/laf/

The companion to a book of the same name, this website offers selected oral history resources that examine lives in Southern textile mill towns from the 1880s to the 1930s. The website is divided into three sections. "Life on the Land" discusses agricultural roots of the rural South, changes in farm labor after the Civil War, and economic factors that caused the transition to mill work in the late nineteenth century. "Mill Village and Factory" describes work in the mills and life in the company mill towns. "Work and Protest" discusses labor protests of the 1920s, formation of unions, and the textile strike of 1934. The website contains fifteen photographs and nearly seventy audio clips drawn from oral history interviews with descendants of millhands and others involved in the history of the Southern textile industry. There are valuable links to Southern history, oral history, and textile mill history websites. This website is ideal for studying rural Southern life and labor history from Reconstruction through the 1930s.

163. Marcus Garvey and Universal Negro Improvement Association Papers Project

James S. Coleman African Studies Center, University of California, Los Angeles
http://www.international.ucla.edu/africa/mgpp/

The life and work of black activist Marcus Garvey (1887–1940) is presented on this website. Garvey was the leader of the Universal Negro Improvement Association

(UNIA), and "champion of the back-to-Africa movement." Materials include forty documents, such as correspondence, editorials, reports of U.S. Department of Justice Bureau of Investigation agents, articles from African American newspapers, and a chapter from Garvey's autobiography. Fifteen background essays accompany the primary documents. The website also provides four audio clips from recordings of speeches Garvey made in 1921 and twenty-four images, including photos of Garvey, his wife, and colleagues, and facsimiles of UNIA documents. These materials are particularly valuable as a condensed history of Garvey's movement as well as for those studying African American political and cultural movements.

164. Margaret Sanger Papers Project

Department of History, New York University
http://www.nyu.edu/projects/sanger/

Selected materials by and about the "birth control pioneer" Margaret Sanger (1879–1966) are provided here. A link to a companion website offers approximately 200 documents dealing with the *The Woman Rebel*, Sanger's 1914 "radical feminist monthly," for which she was indicted and tried for violation of federal obscenity laws. The project plans to digitize more than 600 of Sanger's speeches and articles. At present, there are twenty-five transcribed speeches, 182 newspaper articles from 1911 to 1921, four public statements, a letter written by Sanger in 1915, and more than fifty articles from the *Margaret Sanger Papers Project Newsletter*, some of which contain primary-source materials. There are plans to add to items regularly. Materials also include twenty-seven links to websites offering Sanger writings, a biographical essay, and a bibliography. Links to collections of images and an MP3 file of Margaret Sanger's 1953 "This I Believe" speech are also available.

165. The 1906 San Francisco Earthquake and Fire

Bancroft Library, University of California
http://bancroft.berkeley.edu/collections/earthquakeandfire/splash.html

Created to commemorate the one-hundred-year anniversary of the San Francisco earthquake, this exhibit and archive features an extensive collection of primary-source material, an interactive map, and a 360-degree view of the damage to the city. The primary sources include thousands of images and text files, offering more than eight thousand photographs, five hundred cityscapes, and five hundred letters, as well as a host of additional resources, such as broadsides, oral history texts, periodical articles, photomechanical prints, reports, and stereographs. Visitors can browse the archive by genre or subject or search by keyword, subject, genre, or geographic location. The exhibit has five galleries, each with several text/photograph displays: San Francisco before the fire; the earthquake; the fire, including a map showing burned districts; the story of refugees and survivors; and reconstruction. The interactive map divides San Francisco into ten regions, each of which can be browsed or searched for images taken in that region. It also includes eleven aerial cityscape views. The 360-degree panoramic view of San Francisco shortly after the disaster is composed of eleven separate photographs taken from the roof of the Fairmont Hotel.

166. Performing Arts in America, 1875–1923

New York Public Library for the Performing Arts
http://digital.nypl.org/lpa/nypl/lpa_home4.html

A selection of more than 16,000 items relating to the performing arts of the late nineteenth and early twentieth centuries is offered on this website. Materials include books, clippings, photographs, drawings, music, manuscripts, moving images, photographs, posters and lobby cards, programs, and recorded sound. Diverse types of material on specific performers, such as Ruth St. Denis, Loie Fuller, and Isadora Duncan, have been selected to allow focused study. More than 2,400 entries are available for photographs (entries often contain multiple images), as well as twenty-one large format clippings scrapbooks, each with more than one hundred pages. The website also presents sixteen full-text books and video clips from nine early motion pictures, including a nine-minute clip featuring renowned dancer Anna Pavlova in Lois Weber's *The Dumb Girl of Portici* (1914).

167. Photographs from the *Chicago Daily News*:
1902–1933

American Memory Project, Library of Congress and Chicago Historical Society
http://memory.loc.gov/ammem/ndlpcoop/ichihtml/cdnhome.html

The *Chicago Daily News* was an afternoon paper, sold at a cost of one cent for many years, with stories that tried to appeal to the city's large working-class audience. More than 55,000 photographs taken by *Chicago Daily News* staff photographers dur-

Photograph of young newsboy, 11 August 1904, from *Photographs from the* Chicago Daily News: *1902–1933* [167]. *(Newsboy selling papers, negative #DN-0001753, Chicago Daily News. Photo courtesy of the Chicago History Museum.)*

ing the first decades of the twentieth century are available on this website. Roughly twenty percent of the photos were published in the paper. The website provides subject access to the photographs, which include street scenes, buildings, prominent people, labor violence, political campaigns and conventions, criminals, ethnic groups, workers, children, actors, and disasters. Many photographs of athletes and political leaders are also featured. While most of the images were taken in Chicago and nearby areas, some were taken elsewhere, including at presidential inaugurations. The images provide a glimpse into varied aspects of urban life and document the use of photography by the press during the early twentieth century.

168. Poetic Waves: Angel Island

Garman Yip

http://www.poeticwaves.net/

This small, well-designed website uses a photo tour, profiles, poetry, a timeline, and an image gallery to present the compelling story of the 175,000 Asian immigrants who entered America between 1910 and 1940 through the Angel Island immigration station in California's San Francisco Bay. Many of the immigrants were detained for up to two years at the station. The five-part tour provides an overview and a photographic and video tour of the station's buildings and facilities, along with a description of its operations. "Poetry" allows visitors to listen to and read (in both English and Chinese) five of the many poems that Chinese immigrants carved into the walls of the station's barracks. "People" uses text and audio to tell the individual stories of five immigrants. The timeline covers the history of Angel Island and Asian immigration from 1840 to the present. A small image gallery includes an immigration document, building interiors, a page of interrogation notes, and an image of poetry on barrack walls.

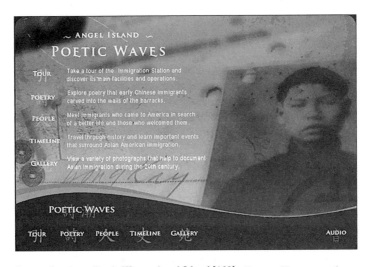

Screenshot from *Poetic Waves: Angel Island* [168]. *(Garman Yip, www.poetic waves.net.)*

169. Prosperity and Thrift: Coolidge Era and the Consumer Economy

American Memory Project, Library of Congress

http://memory.loc.gov/ammem/coolhtml/coolhome.html

This exhibit assembles a wide assortment of materials from the 1920s, items loosely related to the prosperity of the Coolidge years and the rise of a mass consumer economy. The collection includes more than 400 documents, images, and audio and video clips on subjects such as automobiles, consumer goods, department stores, families, *Motion Picture News*, the National Negro Business League, and politics. An introductory essay provides valuable background information on the Coolidge administration with additional insight on the social and cultural context of the era. An alphabetized guide to people, organizations, and topics includes definitions and brief descriptions. This sort of material has not been widely available, and this collection is extremely valuable as a resource for the development of mass consumption.

170. Race and Place: An African-American Community in the Jim Crow South: Charlottesville, VA

Virginia Center for Digital History and Carter G. Woodson Institute of African and Afro-American Studies

http://www.vcdh.virginia.edu/afam/raceandplace/index.html

This archive addresses Jim Crow, or racial segregation, laws from the late 1880s until the mid-twentieth century, focusing on the town of Charlottesville, Virginia. The theme is the connection of race with place by understanding the lives of African Americans in the segregated South. "Political Materials" includes seven political broadsides and a timeline of African American political activity in Charlottesville and Virginia. "Census Data" includes searchable databases containing information about individual African Americans taken from the 1870 and 1910 Charlottesville census records. "City Records" includes information on individual African Americans and African American businesses. "Oral Histories" includes audio files from more than thirty-seven interviews. "Personal Papers" contains indexes to the Benjamin F. Yancey family papers and the letters of Catherine Flanagan Coles. "Newspapers," still in progress, includes more than 1,000 transcribed articles from or about Charlottesville or Albemarle from two major African American newspapers—the *Charlottesville Recorder* and the *Richmond Planet*. "Images" has links to two extensive image collections—the Holsinger Studio Collection and the Jackson Davis Collection of African American Educational Photographs—and three smaller collections.

171. Reclaiming the Everglades: South Florida's Natural History, 1884–1934

American Memory Project, Library of Congress; University of Miami; Florida International University; and Historical Museum of Southern Florida

http://memory.loc.gov/ammem/collections/everglades/

This archive contains primary and secondary sources relating to reclamation efforts of the Everglades and the history of South Florida from 1884 to 1934. Comprising nearly

10,000 pages and images, the compilation includes personal correspondence; government publications, reports, and memos; and images, such as photographs, maps, and postcards. Materials document issues relating to the creation of national parks, including conflicting interests—public, private individual, and corporate—and government accountability. The website also presents a photo exhibit, "The Everglades: Exploitation and Conservation," accompanied by a 1,000-word essay. Two additional features, an interactive timeline and thirty-one biographies of South Florida's most notable personalities, complete this project. This website will be of interest for those

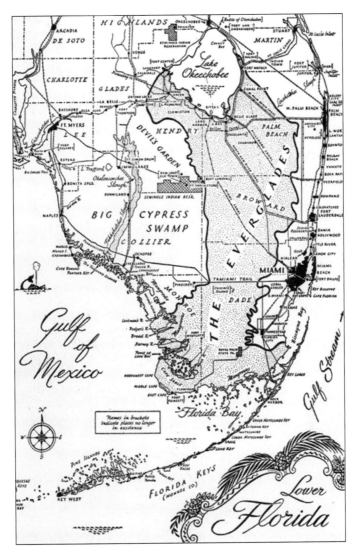

Postcard of the Everglades and Big Cypress, from *Reclaiming the Everglades: South Florida's Natural History, 1884–1934* [171]. *(Postcard of Everglades and Big Cypress, Special Collections, University of Miami Libraries.)*

exploring the establishment of the Everglades National Park, the conservation movement, and the treatment of Native Americans, particularly the Seminoles.

172. Red Hot Jazz Archive: A History of Jazz Before 1930

Scott Alexander

http://www.redhotjazz.com/

Covering more than 200 jazz bands and musicians active from 1895 to 1929, this website offers biographical information, photographs, and audio and video files. It includes more than 200 sound files of jazz recordings by well-known artists, such as Louis Armstrong, Sidney Bechet, and Django Reinhardt, as well as many by dozens of lesser-known musicians. The files are annotated with biographical essays of varying length, discographies, and bibliographic listings. Listings are available for twenty short jazz films made in the late 1920s and early 1930s as well as two video files. Twenty essays and articles about jazz before 1930 come from published liner notes, books, journals, or jazz fans.

173. SIRIS Image Gallery

National Museum of American History, Smithsonian Institution

http://sirismm.si.edu/siris/sirisimagegallery.htm

Highlights from the Smithsonian Institution are presented here, with access to a database of close to 140,000 images from Smithsonian archives and museums. The "Image Gallery" presents a sample of images, browsable by format, such as photographs, slides, drawings, postcards, and stereographs. Images are also organized by repository, including the Freer Gallery, the Archives Center, and the National Anthropological Archive. "Frequently Used Images" provides a link to the most popular images, sorted by month and year. Within the Archives Center, for example, there are four collections with more than 30,000 images, including the "Underwood and Underwood Glass Stereograph Collection, 1895–1921" on topics such as actors, African Americans, disasters, ethnic humor, immigration, Native Americans, labor, presidents, women, and World War I. The "Addison N. Scurlock Collection" presents more than 2,000 black-and-white images, primarily of Washington, D.C., and from African American life. There are 1,500 advertisements from the "Ivory Soap Advertising Collection" and close to two hundred postcards. All images may be searched via the "Search Images" tab (http://siris-archives.si.edu/ipac20/ipac .jsp?profile=allimg).

174. South Texas Border, 1900–1920: Photographs from the Robert Runyon Collection

American Memory Project, Library of Congress and University of Texas, Austin

http://memory.loc.gov/ammem/collections/runyon/

These more than 8,000 images document the history and development of South Texas and the border region. The collection features the life's work of commercial photographer Robert Runyon (1881–1968). Topics include the U.S. military presence in the area prior to and during World War I and the growth and development of

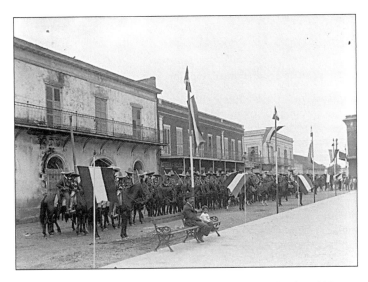

Photograph, Matamoros, Mexico, 1913, from *South Texas Border, 1900–1920: Photographs from the Robert Runyon Collection* [174]. *(Matamoros, Mexico, Robert Runyon Collection, Reproduction Number 00020, The Center for American History, University of Texas. Reprinted with permission.)*

the Rio Grande Valley in the early 1900s. A special section presents nine of Runyon's 350 photographs of the Mexican Revolution (1910–1920) in Matamoros, Monterrey, Ciudad Victoria, and the Texas border area from 1913 through 1916. "Maps of the Lower Rio Grande" offers a number of topographical and military maps depicting the region. The website also offers essays on the revolution and on Runyon.

175. Spanish-American War in Motion Pictures

American Memory Project, Library of Congress
http://memory.loc.gov/ammem/sawhtml/sawhome.html

The Spanish-American War was one of the first wars captured on film. This website features sixty-eight motion pictures of the war and the Philippine Revolution produced by the Edison Manufacturing Company and the American Mutoscope and Biograph Company between 1898 and 1901. The films include footage of troops, ships, notable figures, parades, and battle reenactments shot in the United States, Cuba, and the Philippines. Theodore Roosevelt's Rough Riders are featured alongside footage of the USS *Maine* in Havana harbor. "Special Presentation" puts the motion pictures in chronological order and brief essays provide historical context. "Collection Connections" provides thought-provoking activities and essay topics. This glimpse at early film footage enhances our understanding of the fledgling technology, and offers a way to better understand U.S. imperialism at the turn of the century. The films expose some of the ways in which the birth of cinema emerged alongside, and shaped, changing ideas of gender, race, sexuality, and nation.

176. *Stars and Stripes*: The American Soldiers' Newspaper of World War I, 1918–1919

American Memory Project, Library of Congress
http://memory.loc.gov/ammem/sgphtml/sashtml/

This collection presents the complete run—from February 8, 1918, to June 13, 1919—of the "official newspaper" of the U.S. Army fighting forces during World War I. The American Expeditionary Forces (AEF) were formed in May 1917 following U.S. entrance into the war. General John J. Pershing, the AEF supreme commander, ordered the creation of the *Stars and Stripes* to strengthen morale and promote unity among soldiers. Professionals from the newspaper industry joined the staff, including a few well-known journalists. At its peak, the weekly newspaper reached more than half a million soldiers, providing news of the war, sports reports, cartoons, news from home, and poetry. A special presentation includes essays on the newspaper's contents, staff, advertising, military censorship, the American Expeditionary Forces, and the role women played in the war effort. Search the full text or browse individual issues.

177. Touring Turn-of-the-Century America: Photographs from the Detroit Publishing Company, 1880–1920

American Memory Project, Library of Congress
http://memory.loc.gov/ammem/collections/touring/

The Detroit Publishing Company mass produced photographic images—especially color postcards, prints, and albums—for the American market from the late 1890s to 1924. This collection offers more than 25,000 glass negatives and transparencies and close to 300 color photolithographs from this company. It also includes images taken prior to the company's formation by landscape photographer William Henry Jackson, who became the company's president in 1898. Jackson's work documenting western sites influenced the conservation movement. Although many images were taken in eastern locations, other areas of the United States, the Americas, and Europe are represented. The collection specializes in views of buildings, streets, colleges, universities, natural landmarks, and resorts, as well as copies of paintings. Nearly 300 photographs were taken in Cuba during the Spanish-American War. About 900 mammoth plate photographs include views of Hopi peoples and their crafts and landscapes along several railroad lines in the 1880s and 1890s.

178. Triangle Shirtwaist Factory Fire

Kheel Center for Labor-Management Documentation and Archives, Cornell University
http://www.ilr.cornell.edu/trianglefire/

On March 25, 1911, a fire broke out at the Triangle Shirtwaist Factory in New York City causing the deaths of 148 garment workers—an event that came to be known as one of the hallmark tragedies of the industrial age. This website tells the story of the fire in six chapters: Introduction; Sweatshops and Strikes; Fire; Mourning and Protest; Relief Work; and Investigation, Trial, and Reform. The text, targeted to a middle and high school audience, is accompanied by numerous primary sources that could be of use to more advanced researchers. These include close to seventy photographs, eighteen newspaper articles, seventeen testimonials, three oral histories, excerpts from investigative reports written in the years following the fire, several letters from witnesses, a lecture given by Secretary of Labor Frances Perkins in 1964, and a radio drama re-enacting the event. Accompanying these primary sources is a list of victims and witnesses, a selected bibliography of works surrounding the fire, and tips for writing a paper.

179. Urban Experience in Chicago: Hull-House and Its Neighborhoods, 1889–1963

University of Illinois at Chicago; Jane Addams Hull-House Museum
http://www.uic.edu/jaddams/hull/urbanexp/index.htm

This well-organized website offers more than 900 items related to Hull-House—including newspaper, magazine, and journal articles, letters, memoirs, reports, maps, and photographs. Materials are embedded within a clear historical narrative that illuminates the life of Jane Addams in addition to the history and legacy of Chicago's Hull-House. Users can search the website or focus on any of the one hundred topics arranged in twelve chapters that begin with settlement life in Chicago in the 1880s and end with the movement after Addams's death. Topics include the reform climate in Chicago; activism within the movement; the immigrant experience of race, citizenship, and community; education within the settlement house; and cultural and leisure activities at Hull-House and in Chicago. The website provides a timeline, featuring a pictorial biography of Addams, a geographical section that includes maps of Chicago, and an image section, with twelve photograph sections and essays.

180. Willa Cather Archive

University of Nebraska, Lincoln, Center for Digital Research in the Humanities
http://libtextcenter.unl.edu/cather/index.html

Willa Cather (1873–1947) wrote twelve novels and numerous works of short fiction. She won the Pulitzer Prize in 1923 and is known for her intensive examination of life in the midwestern United States. This extensive archive is dedicated to her life and work. At its core is a collection of all of her novels, short fiction, journalistic writing, interviews, speeches, and public letters published before 1922. All materials are fully searchable. Notably, both *O Pioneers!* and *My Antonia* are accompanied by extensive scholarly notes, historical context, and introductory material. Accompanying her published materials is a collection of 2,054 of Cather's letters (again, annotated and fully searchable), more than 600 photographs of Cather and important people and places in her life, audio of Cather's Pulitzer Prize acceptance speech, and a short video clip of Cather. Several scholarly articles and a text analysis tool are also available.

181. Without Sanctuary: Photographs and Postcards of Lynching in America

James Allen, Collector
http://www.withoutsanctuary.org/

James Allen has assembled a collection of chilling photographs of lynchings throughout America, primarily from the late nineteenth and early twentieth centuries. Many were circulated as souvenir postcards. The website is a companion to Allen's book *Without Sanctuary*. The exhibit can be experienced through a Flash movie with narrative comments by Allen or as a gallery of more than eighty photographs with brief captions. Most images also have links to more extensive descriptions of the circumstances behind each specific act of violence. While the vast majority of lynching victims were African Americans, white victims are also depicted. Individually and as a group, these images are disturbing and difficult to fathom. They provide, however, an excellent resource for approaching the virulence and impact of racism in late nineteenth- and twentieth-century America.

182. *The Wizard of Oz***: An American Fairy Tale**

Library of Congress

http://www.loc.gov/exhibits/oz/

The cultural impact of L. Frank Baum's *The Wonderful Wizard of Oz* is the focus of this well-designed exhibit. Three galleries offer images and explanatory text. "'To Please a Child': L. Frank Baum and the Land of Oz" examines various aspects of the book, including W. W. Denslow's artwork, Baum's original copyright application, and an early review of the book appearing in the October 1900 issue of *The Literary Review*. *To See the Wizard: Oz on Stage and Film* looks at two of the most famous productions of Baum's book, the 1902–1903 stage play that became one of Broadway's greatest successes and the classic 1939 MGM movie, including color posters and a full-page color advertisement placed in the September 1939 issue of *Cosmopolitan*. "To Own the Wizard: Oz Artifacts" examines Oz-related novelties, including *The Wizard of Oz* Monopoly game by Hasbro, a *Wizard of Oz* stamp, and "The Royal Bank of Oz" rebate check from MGM.

Advertising poster for *The Wonderful Wizard of Oz*, 1900, from *The Wizard of Oz:* An American Fairy Tale [182]. *(Library of Congress, Rare Books and Special Collections Division.)*

183. The World of 1898: The Spanish-American War

Hispanic Division, Library of Congress
http://www.loc.gov/rr/hispanic/1898/

This exhibit collects a series of chronologies, images, maps, bibliographies, biographies, essays, and other materials for studying the Spanish-American War. An overview essay discusses the historical context, including events leading up to the war and well-known individuals such as Jose Martí and Theodore Roosevelt. There are four main sections—Cuba, the Philippines, Puerto Rico, and Spain—each presenting an introductory essay, a chronology, and guides to related resources. An index offers short descriptive entries on fifty-seven people; thirteen places in Puerto Rico, Cuba, and the Philippines; and twenty-one events. Also available are a chronology and a selected bibliography of personal narratives, illustration sources, manuscripts, and maps. Finally, there is a list of additional Library of Congress resources and relevant American Memory Project presentations.

184. World War I Document Archive

Jane Plotke, Richard Hacken, Alan Albright, and Michael Shackelford
http://net.lib.byu.edu/~rdh7/wwi/

Hundreds of documents and thousands of images relating to World War I, with particular emphasis on military, diplomatic, and political resources, are available on this website. Documents are arranged chronologically and by type, including more than one hundred official documents from sixteen countries, one hundred personal reminiscences, and twenty-four treaties from 1856 to 1928. A photo archive provides 1,844 images in fifteen categories, including individuals, locations, heads of state, commanders, refugees, and war albums. The website also offers substantial sections on the maritime war and the medical front, an alphabetical bibliographical dictionary with over 200 names, and approximately 125 links to related websites. The authors—volunteers from a World War I electronic discussion network—encourage user participation in expanding the website.

Great Depression and World War II, 1929–1945

185. Ad*Access

Digital Scriptorium, Duke University
http://library.duke.edu/digitalcollections/adaccess/

Images of more than 7,000 advertisements printed primarily in newspapers and magazines in the United States from 1911 to 1955 appear on this well-developed website. The material is drawn from a collection of one of the oldest and largest advertising agencies, the J. Walter Thompson Company. Advertisements are divided into five main subjects areas: "Radio" (including radios, radio parts, and programs), "Television" (including television sets and programs), "Transportation" (including airlines, rental cars, buses, trains, and ships), "Beauty and Hygiene" (including cosmetics, soaps, and shaving supplies), and "World War II" (U.S. government-related, such as V-mail and bond drives).

Ads are searchable by keyword, type of illustration, and special features. A timeline from 1915 to 1955 provides general context. "About Ad Access" furnishes an overview of advertising history, as well as a bibliography and list of advertising repositories.

186. After the Day of Infamy: "Man on the Street" Interviews Following the Attack on Pearl Harbor

American Memory Project, Library of Congress

http://memory.loc.gov/ammem/afcphhtml/afcphhome.html

More than twelve hours of audio interviews conducted in the days following the December 7, 1941, attack on Pearl Harbor and in January and February 1942 are included on this website. Interviews include the voices of 200 "ordinary Americans" recorded in ten places across the United States. December recordings were made by fieldworkers contacted by the Library of Congress Radio Research Project to gather opinions of a diverse group of citizens regarding American entrance into the war. In the 1942 recordings, produced by the Office of Emergency Management, interviewees were instructed to speak their minds directly to the president. Interviewees discuss domestic issues, including racism and labor activism, in addition to the war. Related written documents and biographies of the fieldworkers are also presented. The interviews are available in audio files and text transcriptions, and are searchable by keyword, subject, and location.

187. America from the Great Depression to World War II: Photographs from the FSA-OWI, 1935–1945

American Memory Project, Library of Congress

http://memory.loc.gov/ammem/fsowhome.html

During the New Deal and World War II, a period marked by the impulse to capture in writing, sounds, and images significant aspects of American life and traditions, government photographers with the Farm Security Administration (FSA) and the Office of War Information (OWI) took thousands of pictures. This website features more than 150,000 photographs from this project. The photographs document the ravages of the Great Depression, scenes of everyday life in small towns and cities, and mobilization campaigns for World War II. This website also includes approximately 1,600 color photographs and selections from two popular collections: "'Migrant Mother' Photographs" and "Photographs of Signs Enforcing Racial Discrimination." The website also provides a bibliography, a background essay, portrait samples of eighteen FSA-OWI photographers, and links to five related websites. This is a great source for studying the documentary expression of the 1930s and 1940s.

188. American Life Histories: Manuscripts from the Federal Writers' Project, 1936–1940

American Memory Project, Library of Congress

http://memory.loc.gov/ammem/wpaintro/wpahome.html

Close to 3,000 life histories from 1936 to 1940, compiled and transcribed by the staff of the Folklore Project, are presented here. They are part of the Federal Writers' Project for the U.S. Works Progress (later Work Projects) Administration (WPA). Documents represent the work of more than 300 writers from twenty-four states.

Photograph of women quilting in Box Elder County, Utah, from *America from the Great Depression to World War II: Photographs from the FSA-OWI, 1935–1945* [187]. *(Library of Congress, Prints & Photographs Division, call number LC-USF33-012855-M2.)*

The histories, usually between 2,000 and 15,000 words in length, take the form of narratives, dialogs, reports, and case histories. Drafts and revisions are included. A typical history may offer information on family life, education, income, occupation, political views, religion, mores, medical needs, diet, and observations on society and culture. "Voices from the Thirties," illustrated with photographs of the project's staff at work, interviewees, and their environment, provides contextual information on the creation of the collection. This multifaceted website offers first-hand accounts on subjects such as slavery, nineteenth-century American folk cultures, and the social history of the Great Depression.

189. Ansel Adams's Photographs of Japanese-American
Internment at Manzanar

American Memory Project, Library of Congress
http://memory.loc.gov/ammem/collections/anseladams/

During World War II, the U.S. government forced more than 100,000 Japanese Americans to leave their homes and businesses, relocating them to internment camps from California to Arkansas. Well-known photographer Ansel Adams documented the lives of Japanese Americans at the Manzanar War Relocation Center in California—from portraits to daily life, including agriculture and leisure. This website presents 242 original negatives and 209 photographic prints, often displayed together to show Adams's developing and cropping techniques. His 1944 book on Manzanar, *Born Free and Equal*, is also reproduced. Adams donated the collection to the Library of Congress in 1965, writing, "The purpose of my work was to show how these people, suffering under a great injustice . . . had overcome the sense of defeat and dispair [sic] by building for themselves a vital community in an arid (but magnificent) environment."

Photograph, Roy Takeno, Manzanar Relocation Center,
1943, from *Ansel Adams's Photographs of Japanese-American
Internment at Manzanar* [189]. *(Library of Congress, Prints &
Photographs Division, Ansel Adams, photographer, reproduction number
LC-DIG-pprs-00407 DLC.)*

190. By the People, For the People: Posters from the WPA, 1936–1943

American Memory Project, Library of Congress

http://memory.loc.gov/ammem/wpaposters/wpahome.html

This colorful exhibit showcases more than 900 Work Projects Administration (WPA) posters produced from 1936 to 1943 as part of the New Deal program to support the arts during the Depression. Silkscreen, lithograph, and woodcut posters promoted New Deal and local programs dealing with public health, safety, education, travel and tourism, and community activities, as well as publicizing art exhibits, theater, and musical performances in seventeen states and the District of Columbia. Each poster is accompanied by a brief description. Three special presentations feature more than forty posters, including highlights of the collection's breadth and depth as well as style and content; an audio recording with a silkscreen artist; and a Federal Art Project calendar. A bibliography of ten related scholarly works also is included.

191. Densho: The Japanese American Legacy Project

Densho
http://www.densho.org/

Densho means "to pass on to the next generation." In this quest, this website offers an archive of more than 110 oral histories in 500 hours of video interviews on Japanese American internment during World War II. Materials also include approximately 8,000 historical photographs, documents, and newspapers. Access to archival materials requires free registration. Once registered, users may select materials according to thirty-two topics, including immigration, community, religion and churches, education, race and racism, identity values, resistance, economic losses, redress and reparations, and reflections on the past. Materials available without registration include lesson plans and information on "Causes of the Incarceration," "Civil Rights and Japanese American Incarceration," "Sites of Shame: Japanese American Detention Facilities," and "In the Shadow of My Country: A Japanese American Artist Remembers." The website also offers ninety multimedia materials providing historical context, a timeline, a glossary, and a list of related sources in print and online.

192. Disability History Museum

Disability History Museum
http://www.disabilitymuseum.org/

This ongoing project was designed to present materials on the historical experiences of those with disabilities. The website currently presents nearly 800 documents and more than 930 still images dating from the late eighteenth century to the present. Subjects are organized by category: advocacy, types of disability, government, institutions, medicine, organizations, private life, public life, and personal names. Documents include articles, poems, pamphlets, speeches, letters, book excerpts, and editorials. Of special interest are documents from the Roosevelt Warm Springs Institute for Rehabilitation Archives, including the *Polio Chronicle*, a journal published by patients at Warm Springs, Georgia, from 1931 to 1934. Images include photographs, paintings, postcards, lithographs, children's book illustrations, and nineteenth-century family photographs, as well as postcard views of institutions, beggars, charity events, and types of wheelchairs.

193. Federal Emergency Relief Administration
(FERA) Photographs

University of Washington Libraries
http://content.lib.washington.edu/feraweb/index.html

When President Roosevelt created the Federal Emergency Relief Administration (FERA) in May of 1933, the nation was in the throes of the Great Depression. Roughly fifteen million Americans were unemployed, many of whom had lost both their livelihoods and their life savings. FERA maintained local relief organizations that created work projects for the unemployed, primarily construction and engineering projects. This collection of close to 200 photographs documents the work of FERA in King County, Washington, which includes Seattle, Tacoma, and Bellevue. The bulk of photographs depict construction projects for roads, bridges, schools, public buildings, and parks. Workers also appear working on sewing machines as well as at relief centers, the blacksmiths' forge, the furniture factory, and the sheet metal workshop. Together, these photographs shed light not only on the development of King County, but also on important general aspects of the New Deal program they sought to document.

194. Flint Sit-Down Strike

Historical Voices
http://www.historicalvoices.org/flint

This rich, multimedia resource provides an introduction to "the greatest strike in American history." In 1936–1937, the recently formed United Auto Workers led a six-week occupation of the General Motors plant at Flint, Michigan. Using the new tactic of remaining in the plant rather than picketing outside, the strikers stopped production and won many demands. The website begins with a short introductory essay and a small bibliography and webography. The three main sections—organization, strike, and aftermath—provide nearly one hundred audio interviews recorded between 1978 and 1984 with former strikers recalling work conditions prior to the strike, experiences during the sit-in, the hostile reaction of Flint residents, the role of the Women's Auxiliary, and conditions following the strike. Each section includes a narrative essay. In addition, the website presents slideshows, an audio timeline, and a Flash-generated strike map with textual and audio links.

195. Franklin D. Roosevelt Presidential Library
and Digital Archives

Franklin D. Roosevelt Library and Museum, Marist College
http://www.fdrlibrary.marist.edu/

Offering more than 10,000 documents pertaining to Franklin D. Roosevelt's presidency, this website presents documents that include approximately 6,000 pieces of formerly classified correspondence, reports, and memoranda. Topics include the Atlantic Charter; the United Nations; the Departments of War, Treasury, and State; and the Manhattan Project to develop the atom bomb. The website also offers 1,000 documents pertaining to U.S.-Vatican relations during World War II, 2,000 documents concerning U.S.-German relations, and full texts of thirty "fireside chats." An exhibit examines "The Special Relationship" between Winston Churchill and Roosevelt and the emergence of an Anglo-American alliance. A mini-multimedia showcase contains one video clip of Roosevelt walking and eleven audio clips of speeches. The website also provides information on Eleanor Roosevelt and the Depression, and includes more than 2,000 photographs.

196. Historic Government Publications from
World War II: A Digital Library

Southern Methodist University, Central University Libraries
http://worldwar2.smu.edu

More than 300 U.S. government publications from World War II have been digitized for this website, an ongoing project that plans to add another 200 documents.

Materials include pamphlets and books emphasizing home front issues, such as air raids, preservation, child labor, and victory farms. All materials are searchable by title, author, subject, and keyword. Browsing is also available. A companion collection of photographs, the "Melvin C. Shaffer Collection," depicts the home front situation in Germany, North Africa, Italy, and southern France from 1943 to 1945. Shaffer was a U.S. Army medical photographer assigned to document the medical history of the war through major campaigns; he took the 340 photographs on this website unofficially, with the goal of recording the war's impact on civilians.

197. Historical Thinking Matters

CHNM and Stanford University
http://historicalthinkingmatters.org/

Four guided investigations designed to teach students how to read primary sources and construct historical narratives lie at the heart of this website. The four topics covered are the Spanish-American War, the Scopes Trial, Social Security, and Rosa Parks. Each topic includes a short introductory video, a timeline of events, a central question, and extension activities. For example, the Rosa Parks investigation poses the question: "Why did the boycott of Montgomery's buses succeed?" After completing a simple login, students read annotated documents (including letters written by the boycott organizers, a speech by Martin Luther King Jr., and an interview with a woman working in Montgomery), answer guiding questions, and draw on their responses to answer the question. The website also includes a useful introduction to the idea of historical thinking.

198. The History of Social Security

United States Social Security Administration
http://www.ssa.gov/history/

The Social Security program and the institutional history of the Social Security Administration (SSA) and its contribution to the welfare of the American public are presented on this website. It contains a vast collection of oral histories, audio recordings, and primary documents of SSA. The audio and video clip section includes radio debates on the merits of the Social Security program taped during 1935, Lyndon B. Johnson's remarks on the passage of the Medicare Bill in 1965, and Ronald Reagan's remarks at the signing of the Social Security Amendments of 1983. Also available are Lyndon Johnson and Richard Nixon's recorded telephone conversations that reference Social Security and Medicare. Another notable feature is the thirty-seven oral history interviews conducted by the SSA in the late 1960s and early 1970s. Additional oral history collections are featured, providing information about the 1977 creation of the Health Care Financing Administration and policy issues involving the Medicare and Social Security programs.

199. Medicine and Madison Avenue

Ellen Gartrell, National Humanities Center, and Digital Scriptorium, Duke University
http://library.duke.edu/digitalcollections/mma/

Designed to help users better understand the evolution and complexity of medicinal marketing in the twentieth century, this website provides more than 600 health-related advertisements printed in newspapers and magazines from 1910 to 1960. Ads are organized into six categories: "Household Products," "Over-the-Counter Drugs," "Personal and Oral Hygiene," "Vitamins and Tonics, Food, Nutrition and Diet Aids," "Institutional and Pharmaceutical," and "Cigarettes." The first three categories provide the largest number of advertisements. Supplementary materials, such as internal reports from marketing companies, American Medical Association reports and editorials, Federal Trade Commission archival records, transcripts of 1930s radio commercials, and medical journal articles, focus on the production and influence of health-related advertisements. A bibliography provides eighty further reading suggestions. The project highlights materials for case studies on Fleischmann's Yeast, Listerine, and Scott Tissue.

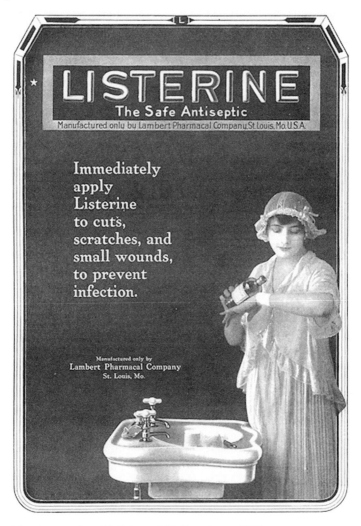

Advertisement from *Medicine and Madison Avenue* [199]. *(Reprinted with permission of Listerine® a registered trademark of Johnson & Johnson. Medicine and Madison Ave. online project, Ad #MM0600, John W. Hartman Center for Sales, Advertising & Marketing History, Rare Book, Manuscript & Special Collections Library, Duke University.)*

Photograph, Elanto Cooperative Store, from the *New Deal Network* [200].
(National Archives and Records Administration, Washington, DC, control number RG69, Negative 21155-D.)

200. New Deal Network

Franklin and Eleanor Roosevelt Institute and Institute for Learning Technologies, Teachers College, Columbia University

http://newdeal.feri.org/

Offering more than 20,000 items, this website focuses on objects, documents, and images relevant to the New Deal. "Document Library" contains more than 900 newspaper and journal articles, speeches, letters, reports, advertisements, and other textual materials that treat a broad array of subjects. They place special emphasis on relief agencies and issues relating to labor, education, agriculture, the Supreme Court, and African Americans. "Photo Gallery" presents more than 5,000 images. "The Magpie Sings the Depression" includes poems, articles, short stories, and graphics from a Bronx high school journal. "Dear Mrs. Roosevelt" highlights letters written by young people to the first lady. Photographs, graphics, cartoons, memoirs, autobiographical essays, and a 20,000-word essay on campus radicalism complete the "Student Activism in the 1930s" section. The website also provides speeches and articles by Henry Wallace, a photo-documentary on a small Alabama town, and materials on the Federal Theatre Project, Tennessee Valley Authority, the Civilian Conservation Corps, and the National Youth Administration.

201. Northwestern European Military Situation Maps from World War II

American Memory Project, Library of Congress

http://memory.loc.gov/ammem/collections/maps/wwii/

Created by the First U.S. Army Group and the Twelfth U.S. Army Group, this collection consists of 416 situation maps from World War II. The maps show the daily

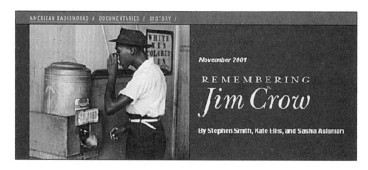

Screenshot from *Remembering Jim Crow* [202]. *(Remembering Jim Crow (American Radio Works) documentary. Courtesy of American Public Media and © Bettmann/CORBIS.)*

positions of allied army units during the campaigns in Western Europe, from the D-Day invasion on June 6, 1944, through Allied occupation on July 26, 1945. There are also more than one hundred reports from the campaigns. Maps offer insight into daily activities, but also a broad view of movement over time. In addition, they highlight the incomplete nature of information available to commanders in the field during wartime. Visitors can search the collection or browse the maps and reports by title, creator, subject, place, or date, and select a zoom level and window size for viewing maps. The website also includes an interactive essay on the Battle of the Bulge.

202. Remembering Jim Crow

American RadioWorks

http://americanradioworks.publicradio.org/features/remembering/

Created as a companion to a National Public Radio (NPR) documentary on segregation in the South, this website presents thirty audio excerpts from oral history interviews, ranging from one minute to ten minutes in length, and 130 photographs. Materials are arranged in six thematically organized sections that address legal, social, and cultural aspects of segregation, black community, and black resistance to the Jim Crow way of life. As anthropologist Kate Ellis, one of the website's creators, notes, the interviews display a "marked contrast between African American and white reflections on Jim Crow." Many of the photographs come from personal collections of the people interviewed. The website presents sixteen photographs taken by Farm Security Administration photographer Russell Lee in New Iberia, Louisiana. Also available are audio files and transcripts of the original radio documentary, more than ninety additional stories, a sampling of state segregation laws arranged by topic, links to nine related websites, and a bibliography.

203. Southern Mosaic: The John and Ruby Lomax
1939 Southern States Recording Trip

American Memory Project, Library of Congress

http://memory.loc.gov/ammem/lohtml/lohome.html

In 1939, John Lomax, curator of the Library of Congress Archive of American Folk Song, and his wife Ruby Terrill Lomax, embarked on a 6,500-mile journey through the South. During their travels, they recorded more than 700 folk tunes that now are available as audio files on this website. Genres include ballads, blues, children's songs, cowboy songs, fiddle tunes, field hollers, lullabies, play-party songs, spirituals, and work songs. The website also presents field notes containing personal information on some of the more than 300 performers the Lomaxes recorded, notes on geography and culture, and excerpts from correspondence. More than fifty letters to and from the Lomaxes, 380 photographs, a bibliography of twenty-two works, and a map are also offered. The website is keyword searchable and can be browsed by subject as well as title, song text, and performer.

204. Studs Terkel: Conversations with America

Chicago Historical Society
http://www.studsterkel.org/index.html

Created to honor Studs Terkel, the noted oral historian, radio host, and Pulitzer Prize–winning author, this website makes available more than 400 audio clips of interviews Terkel conducted over fifty years. The seven galleries explore a variety of subjects, including organized labor, the 1929 stock market crash, New Deal programs, World War II, Hiroshima, folk music, race relations, politics, and urban life in Chicago. The interviews present well-known figures as well as ordinary voices, such as people traveling by train to the March on Washington in 1963. Complementing these interviews is a one-hour video interview with Terkel in which he emphasizes the importance of accurate knowledge about the past. An educational section addresses the use of oral history in the classroom. This well-designed website is valuable for studying the Great Depression, World War II, race relations, and labor issues.

205. *Time* Archive, 1923 to Present

Time *Magazine*
http://www.time.com/time/coversearch

Time magazine published its first edition on March 23, 1923. Updated on a regular basis, this website endeavors to feature all *Time* magazine covers published since that first issue. Covers can be searched by keyword or browsed by year. Exploring *Time* covers from the early years shows that individuals (generally men in political leadership positions) were favored up until the late 1960s. Indeed, House of Representatives Speaker Joseph G. Cannon occupies *Time*'s first cover, China's General Chiang Kai-shek appears several times between the late 1920s and 1940s, African leaders surface at decolonization in the late 1950s, and Ralph Nader can be found trumpeting the "consumer revolt" on a cover from December 1969. Those interested in U.S. foreign policy (search China, Russia, Vietnam, or Latin America), popular culture and entertainment, the environment, religion, and legal history also will find valuable resources. Within each keyword search, suggestions for related topics are helpful.

206. U.S. Holocaust Memorial Museum

U.S. Holocaust Memorial Museum
http://www.ushmm.org

Interactive exhibitions and resources address the Holocaust and related subjects. The website is composed of five sections: "Education," "Research," "History,"

Photograph of surviving children being liberated from a concentration camp
from the *U.S. Holocaust Memorial Museum* [206]. *(United States Holocaust
Memorial Museum.)*

"Remembrance," and "Conscience." "Education" introduces the subject of the
Holocaust and provides extensive bibliographies. "Research" contains a survivor
registry and an international directory of activities relating to Holocaust-era assets.
Searchable catalogs pertaining to the museum's collections and library are easy to
navigate, and provide artworks, artifacts, documents, photographs, films, videos,
oral histories, and music. "History" includes the Holocaust Learning Center, with
images, essays, and documents on seventy-five subjects, such as anti-Semitism,
refugees, pogroms, extermination camps, and resistance. "Conscience" contains
information on current genocidal practices in Sudan.

207. Voices from the Dust Bowl: The Charles L. Todd and Robert Sonkin Migrant Worker Collection, 1940–1941

American Memory Project, Library of Congress
http://memory.loc.gov/ammem/afctshtml/tshome.html

These materials examine Depression-era migrant work camps in central California.
The Farm Security Administration (FSA) managed the camps that were primarily
inhabited by migrants from the rural areas of Oklahoma and nearby states. Materials
include 371 audio recordings of songs, interviews, and camp announcements, and
transcriptions of 113 songs. Print and image materials include twenty-three photographs, newspaper clippings, and eleven camp newsletters. Additional materials
address the role of the ethnographer, including a Works Progress Administration
folk song questionnaire; the field notes and correspondence of Charles L. Todd and
Robert Sonkin, the original collectors of the materials; and two published magazine
articles by Todd. Topics range from camp court proceedings and personal narratives to square dances and baseball games. The website also includes a bibliography,
a background essay, and an essay on the recording expedition. This is a valuable

website for the study of Depression-era migrants, their folk traditions, and the documentary impulse of the period.

208. William P. Gottlieb: Photographs from the Golden Age of Jazz

American Memory Project, Library of Congress
http://memory.loc.gov/ammem/wghtml/wghome.html

Writer-photographer William P. Gottlieb (1917–2006) documented the New York and Washington, D.C., jazz scene from 1938 to 1948 through more than 1,600 photographs. During the course of his career, Gottlieb took portraits of prominent jazz musicians—including Louis Armstrong, Duke Ellington, Charlie Parker, Billie Holiday, Dizzy Gillespie, Earl Hines, Thelonious Monk, Ella Fitzgerald, and Benny Carter—and legendary venues, such as 52nd Street, the Apollo Theatre, Cafe Society, the Starlight Roof, and Zanzibar. The website also features approximately 170 related articles by Gottlieb from *Down Beat* magazine; sixteen photographs accompanied by Gottlieb's audio commentary on various assignments; a 4,300-word biography based on oral histories; and a thirty-one-title bibliography. Extremely valuable for jazz fans, music historians, musicians, and those interested in urban popular culture.

Postwar United States, 1945 to the Early 1970s

209. *Brown* v. *Board of Education*

The University of Michigan Library Digital Archive
http://www.lib.umich.edu/exhibits/brownarchive/index.html

Created in anticipation of the fifty-year anniversary of the monumental Supreme Court decision of *Brown* v. *Board of Education*, this website covers four general areas: Supreme Court cases, busing and school integration, school integration in Ann Arbor (home of the University of Michigan), and recent re-segregation trends in America. The website contains a case summary and the Court's opinion for each of thirty-four landmark court cases, from *Plessy* v. *Ferguson* to *Brown* v. *Board of Education of Topeka*. *Brown* includes transcripts of oral arguments as well. Visitors can also read the oral histories of five members of the University of Michigan community who remember the *Brown* decision and its impact. There are more than thirty photographs of participants in the *Brown* case and other civil rights activists, as well as a collection of documents pertaining to desegregation in the Ann Arbor Public School District. A statistical section details the growing number of African Americans in Michigan and Ann Arbor schools from 1950 to 1960.

210. Central High Crisis: Little Rock, 1957

Little Rock Newspapers, Inc.
http://www.ardemgaz.com/prev/central/

This collection of newspaper articles and photographs from two Arkansas newspapers explores the 1957 crisis in the city of Little Rock. National attention focused on the city when Governor Orval Faubus refused to allow nine African American students to desegregate the city's all-white Central High School, despite federal court rulings to the contrary. In response, President Dwight D. Eisenhower reluctantly became the first president since Reconstruction to send federal troops to protect the rights of African Americans. Materials include news articles and editorials from each day of the month-long crisis, articles on the anniversaries from 1997 to 2000, and sixteen photographs. In addition, material on the fortieth anniversary of the crisis is provided: nineteen op-ed pieces, speeches, an interview with President Clinton, timelines, and a 1991 defense by Faubus of his actions.

211. CIA Electronic Reading Room

Central Intelligence Agency (CIA)
http://www.foia.cia.gov/default.asp

The Central Intelligence Agency (CIA) has digitized thousands of formerly secret documents declassified to comply with Freedom of Information Act requests. Keyword search capabilities are provided for the complete website. In addition, there are eight collections designated as "frequently requested records" that total nearly 8,000 documents. These collections cover a number of Cold War topics: CIA involvement in the 1954 coup in Guatemala, convicted spies Ethel and Julius Rosenberg, the 1961 Bay of Pigs affair, and two well-known espionage incidents. Additional topics include POW–MIAs in Vietnam, human rights abuses in Latin America, and UFOs. A disclaimer notes that some material cannot be disclosed due to national security laws, and released pages often have material deleted or blacked out. Still, the material offered is voluminous and useful for studying Cold War foreign policy and military history.

212. Civil Rights in Mississippi Digital Archive

University of Southern Mississippi Libraries and Center for Oral History
http://www.lib.usm.edu/legacy/spcol/crda/

These 150 oral history interviews and sixteen collections of documents address the civil rights movement in Mississippi. Interviews were conducted with figures on both sides of the movement, including volunteers and activists as well as "race-baiting" Governor Ross Barnett and national White Citizens Council leader William J. Simmons. Document collections offer hundreds of pages of letters, journals, photographs, pamphlets, newsletters, FBI reports, and arrest records. Approximately twenty-five interviews also offer audio clips. Users may browse finding aids or search by keyword. Six collections pertain to Freedom Summer, the 1964 volunteer initiative in Mississippi to establish schools, register voters, and organize a bi-racial Democratic party. One collection is devoted to the freedom riders who challenged segregation in 1961. Four explanatory essays provide historical context. Short biographies are furnished on each interviewee and donor, as well as a list of topics addressed and thirty links to other civil rights websites.

213. CWIHP: Cold War International History Project

Woodrow Wilson International Center for Scholars

http://www.wilsoncenter.org/index.cfm?fuseaction=topics.home&topic_id=1409

Scholarship on the Cold War has been written primarily by Westerners with little access to sources in Soviet archives. This extensive collection seeks to remedy this gap in Cold War historiography by presenting sources from the former Communist bloc. Thousands of documents in the diplomatic history of the Cold War are currently available, stretching in time from the 1945–1946 Soviet occupation of northern Iran through the late 1990s. The annotated sources are divided into fifty collections and by geographic region. Collections cover a wide range of topics, including specific events (1954 Geneva Conference on Indochina, 1956 Hungarian Revolution, 1980–1981 Polish Crisis) and broader topics stretching over longer periods of time (Economic Cold War, Nuclear Non-Proliferation, the Cold War in Africa). Collections vary widely in size, between three and several hundred documents, and include primarily official documents and communication—meeting minutes, memoranda, transcribed conversations between leaders, reports, and several personal letters and diary entries.

214. Dynamics of Idealism: Volunteers for Civil Rights, 1965–1982

Data and Program Library Service, Michael T. Aiken, N. J. Demereth III, Gerald Marwell, Sociology Department, University of Wisconsin-Madison

http://www.disc.wisc.edu/Idealism/index.html

These materials were collected for a study on the attitudes, backgrounds, goals, and experiences of volunteers participating in a 1965 Southern Christian Leadership Conference voter registration effort. Resources include questionnaires submitted prior to and following the project, as well as a follow-up survey conducted in 1982. Participants were queried about why they volunteered, what they expected, their attitudes regarding race and politics, images they held of the South, expectations they had regarding the African American community, personal memories and effects of their participation, and subsequent attitudes regarding civil rights, violence, and social change. These resources offer insight into the civil rights movement and some sociological aspects of American reformers.

215. Experiencing War: Stories from the Veterans History Project

Library of Congress, American Folklife Center

http://www.loc.gov/vets/

This collection presents video and audio oral histories and additional material from American veterans of twentieth-century wars. Materials include memoirs (some lengthy), letters, diaries, photo albums, scrapbooks, poetry, artwork, and official documents. The website currently provides digital materials from 4,351 veterans from World War I, World War II, the Korean War, the Vietnam War, the Persian Gulf War, the war in Afghanistan, the Iraq War, and other similar events. The 226 video interviews range from twenty-five minutes to two hours in length. The material presented is part of a rapidly growing archive, the *Veterans History Project*, created by Congress in 2000 to collect stories from the nineteen million living veterans. Other sections highlight World War I; World War II's forgotten theaters in China, Burma, and India; and thirty-seven other unique war experiences.

216. Frontera Collection of Mexican American Music

Arhoolie Foundation, UCLA Chicano Research Studies Center,
UCLA Music Library & Digital Library Program, Los Tigres Del Norte Foundation
http://digital.library.ucla.edu/frontera/

This collection of commercially produced Mexican American vernacular music is the largest of its kind, with more than 100,000 recordings. The music, originally published between 1905 and the 1990s, is primarily in Spanish. This website presents digitized versions of roughly 30,000 recordings. The music ranges widely in style and includes lyric songs, *canciones, boleros, rancheras, sones,* instrumental music, and the first recordings of *norte* and *conjunto* music, as well as politically motivated speeches and comedy skits. A browsable list of subjects shows that love (unrequited love, adultery, regrets), war (Korean War, Mexican Revolution, World Wars I and II), and praise (of country, guitar, mother) are common themes in the collection. Unfortunately, the songs are available to the general public only in fifty-second sound clips. Users interested in gaining full access to a select group of songs for research are encouraged to contact the website's administrators.

217. History and Politics Out Loud

Jerry Goldman, Northwestern University
http://www.hpol.org/

Audio materials on this website were designed to capture "significant political and historical events and personalities of the twentieth century." Materials include 107 items, including speeches, addresses, and private telephone conversations from nineteen speakers. Most material comes from three U.S. presidents: Richard M. Nixon (thirty-four items), Lyndon Baines Johnson (thirty items), and John F. Kennedy (nineteen items). Additional material highlights international figures such as Secretary of State George Marshall; British Prime Minister Winston Churchill; civil rights leaders Martin Luther King Jr., John Lewis, and A. Philip Randolph; Supreme Court Justices William O. Douglas, Arthur J. Goldberg, and Oliver Wendell Holmes Jr.; and Soviet Union Premier Nikita S. Khrushchev. This website provides an opportunity to experience the persuasive speaking powers of twentieth-century world leaders.

218. Internet Moving Images Archive

Rick Prelinger, Prelinger Archives and Internet Archive
http://www.archive.org/details/prelinger

A privately held collection of twentieth-century American ephemeral films, produced for specific purposes and not intended for long-term survival, are presented here. The website contains nearly 2,000 high-quality digital video files documenting various aspects of twentieth-century American culture, society, leisure, history, industry, technology, and landscape. It includes films produced between 1927 and 1987 by and for U.S. corporations, nonprofit organizations, trade associations, community and interest groups, and educational institutions. More than eighty films address Cold War issues. Films depict ordinary people in normal daily activities such as working, dishwashing, driving, and learning proper behavior, in addition to treating such subjects as education, health, immigration, nuclear energy, social issues, and religion. The website contains an index of 403 categories. This is an important source for studying business history, advertising, cinema studies, the Cold War, and twentieth-century American cultural history.

219. Literature and Culture of the American 1950s

Al Filreis, University of Pennsylvania
http://writing.upenn.edu/~afilreis/50s/home.html

This collection of more than one hundred primary texts, essays, biographical sketches, obituaries, book reviews, and partially annotated links explores the cultural, intellectual, and political trends of the 1950s. Organized alphabetically and according to lesson plans, this eclectic collection of readings is structured around a few landmark texts and topics, including McCarthyism and anticommunism, Daniel Bell's *The End of Ideology* (1960), William H. Whyte's *The Organization Man* (1956), feminism, Philip Rieff's *The Triumph of the Therapeutic* (1966), and conformity in universities. Materials include substantial excerpts from Vance Packard's *The Status Seekers* (1959) and the *Encyclopedia of the American Left*, in addition to retrospective analyses of the postwar period.

220. Lyndon Baines Johnson Library and Museum

Lyndon Baines Johnson Library and Museum
http://www.lbjlib.utexas.edu/

The heart of this collection about President Lyndon Baines Johnson is a group of seventy-seven oral history interviews (up to 200 pages each) with members of Johnson's administration, congressional colleagues, journalists, civil rights leaders, and a historian. The website provides fourteen audio files, including telephone conversations, State of the Union addresses, Johnson's speech to Congress following the Kennedy assassination, and an excerpt of his television address announcing his decision not to run for a second term. Also available are transcripts of twenty-five speeches, fifty days of diary entries, and the ninety-nine National Security Action memoranda issued during Johnson's presidency relaying foreign policy directives and initiating actions. There are 150 photographs and one campaign advertisement. Biographical information is furnished in two chronologies. An exhibit from the Johnson Museum provides an essay about events in Johnson's lifetime.

221. Martin Luther King, Jr., Papers Project

Stanford University
http://www.stanford.edu/group/King/

Featuring texts by and about Martin Luther King Jr., this regularly updated website currently contains more than 1,400 speeches, sermons, and other writings, mostly

Screenshot from *Martin Luther King, Jr., Papers Project* [221].

taken from five volumes covering the period from 1929 to 1968. These are listed in the "Published Documents" section under "Papers." In addition, sixteen chapters of materials published in 1998 as *The Autobiography of Martin Luther King, Jr.* are available. The website presents important sermons and speeches from later periods, including "Letter from a Birmingham Jail," the March on Washington address, the Nobel Peace Prize acceptance speech, and "Beyond Vietnam." Additional materials include an interactive chronology of King's life, two biographical essays, more than twenty audio files of recorded speeches and sermons, and twelve articles on King. More than thirty photographs complete the website. The *King Papers Project* is valuable for studying King's views and discourse on civil rights, race relations, non-violence, education, peace, and other political, religious, and philosophical topics.

222. National Election Studies

National Election Studies

http://www.electionstudies.org/

This wealth of data presents National Election Studies surveys of the American electorate conducted in presidential and congressional election years from 1948 to 2006. Large files of raw data can be downloaded. In addition, *The ANES Guide to Public Opinion and Electoral Behavior* is available and is readily accessible. Composed of more than one hundred tables and graphs, the guide traces nine key variables in the makeup and opinions of the electorate. These include social and religious characteristics, partisanship and evaluation of political parties, ideological self-identification, public opinion on public policy issues, support for the political system, political involvement and partisanship, evaluation of presidential candidates, evaluation of congressional candidates, and vote choice. This website also provides pilot studies on recent surveying issues, such as measuring exposure to television advertisements, and a 5,000-item bibliography.

223. NSA and the Cuban Missile Crisis

National Security Agency (NSA)

http://www.nsa.gov/cuba/

This website provides access to facsimiles of one hundred declassified documents relating to the Cuban Missile Crisis. Documents include reports from Signal and Communications Intelligence and NSA memos, twenty written by the Director of National Security. For example, the first document from 1960 is entitled "Indications of Soviet arms shipments to Cuba, weekly COMINT Economic Briefing." Documents are indexed by date and include brief descriptions. The documents describe Soviet involvement in Cuba and Cuban military activities by year, focusing on 1960, 1961, 1962, 1963, and 1969. This website also provides a synopsis of the crisis, emphasizing the Cuban arms buildup, the growing crisis, and the moments of crisis.

224. Parallel History Project on Cooperative Security

Parallel History Project

http://www.php.isn.ethz.ch/collections/index.cfm

These more than 350 recently declassified documents from archives of former Warsaw Pact countries and the United States reveal previously hidden aspects of Cold War military strategy. The project offers documents and accompanying analyses in six categories: Warsaw Pact records; Warsaw Pact war plans; NATO records (U.S. and British); national perspectives (Bulgaria, Romania, Hungary, China, and Poland); crises (Berlin and Libya); and intelligence. The website also provides thirteen oral history interviews with former officials, including two Eisenhower administration officers involved with NATO planning and nuclear weapons policies. Documents reveal a 1964 Warsaw Pact war plan for using nuclear weapons in a preemptive strike against NATO forces and a 1965 Hungarian Army exercise detailing the targeted destruction of Western cities, including Vienna, Munich, Verona, and Vicenza. A thirty-page survey article assesses new histories written since the release of recent documents.

225. Profiles in Science

National Library of Medicine

http://profiles.nlm.nih.gov/

These documents, exhibits, photographs, and essays tell the history of twenty-six prominent twentieth-century scientists, physicians, and experts in biomedical research and public health. The website is divided thematically into "Biomedical Research," "Health and Medicine," and "Fostering Science and Health." The collections include published and unpublished items, such as books, journals, pamphlets, diaries, letters, manuscripts, photographs, audiotapes, video clips, and other materials. Each exhibit includes introductory narratives and biographies of each scientist and a selection of noteworthy documents. The collections are particularly strong in cellular biology, genetics, and biochemistry, with attention to health and medical research policy, application of computers in medicine, science education, and the history of modern science.

226. Rutgers Oral History Archives

Sandra Stewart Holyoak, Rutgers University
http://oralhistory.rutgers.edu

The voices of men and women who served overseas and on the home front during World War II, the Korean War, the Vietnam War, and the Cold War are collected in these oral histories. The project's goal is to learn more about these wars from the perspective of ordinary people. The archive contains 444 full-text interviews, primarily of Rutgers College and Douglass College (formerly New Jersey College for Women) alumni. Rutgers undergraduate students conducted many of the interviews. Interviewees were selected to investigate the effects of the G.I. Bill on American society. The easily navigable website provides an alphabetical interview list with the name of each interviewee, date and place of interview, college of affiliation and class year, theater in which the interviewee served, and branch of service, if applicable. The list also provides "Description" codes, including military occupations such as infantry and artillery members, nurses, and civilian occupations.

227. Seattle Civil Rights and Labor History Project

James N. Gregory, University of Washington
http://depts.washington.edu/civilr/

The long history of struggle for equal rights by various ethnic groups in Seattle, including Filipino, Chinese, Japanese and Native Americans, Jews, Latinos, and African Americans, is documented on this website. Primary and secondary sources integrate labor rights movements with struggles for political rights, as is evident in the "special sections" that highlight the Chicano/a movement, the Black Panther Party, Filipino Cannery Unionism, the United Construction Workers Association, Communism, and the United Farm Workers. Each section brings together oral histories, documents, newspapers, and photographs that are accompanied by written and video commentary to provide historical context. The collection of more than seventy oral histories of activists is especially useful for understanding the lived experience of racism and its especially subtle workings in the Pacific Northwest. Together, these resources provide important national context for the civil rights struggle, too often understood as a solely Southern phenomenon.

228. Television News of the Civil Rights Era

Will Thomas, University of Virginia
http://www.vcdh.virginia.edu/civilrightstv/index.html

In the 1950s and 1960s, the civil rights movement was covered on news stations around the country. This website provides 230 of these video clips from two local television stations in Roanoke, Virginia. Clips feature both national events, such as the speeches of Martin Luther King Jr. and John F. Kennedy, as well as footage of local school desegregation, protests, and interviews on the street. Accompanying this footage are fourteen oral histories (several from Virginians with first-hand knowledge of the Prince Edward Public Schools closing), and twenty-three documents that chronicle the official development of Massive Resistance in Virginia, in particular the involvement of Senator Harry F. Byrd. "Essays and Interpretation" provides important historical context and analysis, with detailed pieces on "Virginia's Massive Resistance to School Desegregation" and the development of television news coverage of the civil rights movement in Virginia and Mississippi.

229. Truman Presidential Museum and Library

Harry S. Truman Library
http://www.trumanlibrary.org/library.htm

The presidency of Harry S. Truman is addressed through these hundreds of government documents, oral histories, photographs, and political cartoons. Materials are organized into twelve central areas: the Berlin airlift, the decision to drop the atomic bomb, desegregation of the Armed Forces, the election campaign of 1948, the Korean War, the Marshall Plan, NATO, the Truman Doctrine, Truman's Farewell Address, recognition of the state of Israel, the United Nations, and the incarceration of Japanese Americans during World War II. Transcripts are available for approximately 120 oral histories conducted with members of Truman's administration and officials from other countries on the Korean War. The website also offers the full text of Truman's diary from 1947; twenty audio files with extracts of speeches, press conferences, and interviews; 122 biographical photographs; and thirty-four political cartoons.

230. White House Tapes: The Presidential
Recordings Program

Miller Center of Public Affairs, University of Virginia
http://millercenter.org/academic/presidentialrecordings/

Close to 5,000 hours of White House meetings and conversations by six American presidents were recorded between 1940 and 1973 and much of the material is available on this website. Presidents include Franklin Roosevelt (eight hours), Harry Truman (ten hours), Dwight Eisenhower (four and a half hours), John Kennedy (193 hours), Lyndon Johnson (550 hours), and Richard Nixon (2,019 hours). A substantial introduction to each set of recordings is provided and edited transcriptions of the Kennedy tapes are available. "Transcripts & Virtual Exhibits" leads to a searchable list of transcripts, tapes (sorted by president), and ten exhibits. Exhibits present short scholarly essays on such topics as the civil rights movement, the Vietnam War, Johnson's "War on Poverty," and the Space Race. Additionally, the site presents sixteen pre-selected multimedia clips that include recordings of Kennedy discussing withdrawal from Vietnam, Johnson talking to McNamara about leaks, Johnson discussing women in politics, and Nixon discussing Mark Felt during the Watergate cover-up.

231. Women in Journalism

Washington Press Club Foundation
http://wpcf.org/oralhistory/ohhome.html

Forty-four "full-life" interviews with American women journalists are available on this website. Interviewees include women who began their careers in the 1920s through the present. Print, radio, and television journalism all are represented. Interviews address difficulties women have encountered entering the profession and how their presence has changed the field. They also discuss political life; famous people interviewed, such as Eleanor Roosevelt; and social, ethical, and technological changes of the twentieth century. A preface and an explanation of methodology introduce the website. Each interview is linked to a photograph and brief biographical sketch of the interviewee. Interviews range from one to twelve sessions and each session is about twenty pages long. Interviews are indexed but not searchable.

Notes, Harry S. Truman, decision to drop atomic bomb, from the *Truman Presidential Museum and Library* [229]. *(Courtesy of the Harry S. Truman Library & Museum.)*

Contemporary United States, 1968 to Present

232. AIDS at 20

New York Times

http://www.nytimes.com/library/national/science/aids/aids-index.html

A 1981 reference to an unusual pneumonia in Los Angeles, California, by the Centers for Disease Control and Prevention marked the beginning of public discussion of the Acquired Immunodeficiency Syndrome, known as AIDS. More than 350 selected *New York Times* articles from 1981 to 2001 related to the AIDS epidemic are available on this website. Materials also include nine articles specifically related to the course of the epidemic's devastation in Africa. There are nine videos, six multimedia presentations, five fact sheets, and four in-depth reports on such subjects as HIV medications, AIDS in New York City, HIV and teens, women and AIDS, the federal response to the crisis, and the history of AIDS. The in-depth reports cover a diverse range of people affected by AIDS, including those of different ethnic backgrounds, and span a wide range of locations within the United States, including rural and urban areas.

Page from *AIDS at 20*, 5 June 2001 [232]. *(From the New York Times, June 5, 2001. All rights reserved. Used by permission and protected by the Copyright Laws of the United States. The printing, copying, redistribution, or retransmission of the material without express written permission is prohibited.)*

233. Bureau of Economic Analysis

U.S. Department of Commerce, Economics and Statistics Administration
http://www.bea.gov/

Comprehensive and summary data estimates concerning national, international, and regional economic activity are available on this website. Additional data is available according to industry. An overview of the economy provides data on production, purchases by type, prices, personal income, government finances, inventories, and balance of payments. An easy-to-use keyword index to a set of annual and quarterly national income and product account (NIPA) tables from 1929 to 2006—found in the "National" section under "Personal Income and Outlays"—allows users access to data on specific product sales and ways that consumers have spent money. Forty-nine recent research papers by staff members address issues such as globalization, how the "new economy" is measured, and structural change of the economy over a twenty-eight-year period.

234. Business Plan Archive

Library of Congress; Center for History and New Media; University of Maryland Libraries
http://www.businessplanarchive.org/

A collection of business plans and planning information, this archive documents the "birth of the Dot Com Era." Documents can be browsed (free registration required) by alphabetical listing of companies, document type, market sector, or market audience, or the archive can be searched by company name. An advanced search option is also available. Currently, there are 2,445 companies in the archive with one or more documents and more than 3,400 archived documents. Each company record includes a brief description of the company, historical information on the company (if available), and related documents. "What We Can Learn" offers three articles on the kinds of observations we can extract from the dot com boom and bust. "Research Corner" offers tips on using the archive in the classroom, announcements, and other project news. Of particular interest are the entries on guidelines and recommendations for studying companies and for using the archive.

235. CQ Historic Documents Series: Online Edition

Congressional Quarterly Press
http://www.cqpress.com/product/CQ-Online-Editions-Historic-Documents.html

Each year since 1972, CQ Press has published a book of one hundred significant documents in U.S. history accompanied by detailed annotations. The entire collection is available on this website, allowing for detailed keyword searching. Documents include U.S. presidential speeches, government and international organization publications, legal decisions, scientific findings, and cultural discussions. The documents are grouped by year and by topic. Topics include the economy, defense, the environment, health care, international affairs, and life in America. A "Favorite Documents" feature allows users to mark and collect documents of interest, and a "CiteNow!" feature provides citations on demand. Though the depth of documents on any one topic is minimal, this website provides an overview of important events in a given year as well as U.S. perception of and response to topics over time.

236. Fifty Years of Coca-Cola Television Advertisements

American Memory Project, Library of Congress

http://memory.loc.gov/ammem/ccmphtml/colahome.html

Highlights of Coca-Cola television advertisements from the Library of Congress Motion Picture archives are exhibited on this website, with fifty commercials, broadcast outtakes, and experimental footage. There are five examples of stop-motion advertisements from the mid-1950s, eighteen experiments with color and lighting for television ads from 1964, and well-known commercials, such as the "Hilltop" commercial featuring the song "I'd Like to Buy the World a Coke" (1971). Additional resources include the "Mean Joe Greene" commercial (1979); the first "Polar Bear" commercial (1993); the "Snowflake" commercial (1999); and "First Experience," an international commercial filmed in Morocco (1999). The website also includes a bibliography and links to finding aids for other television commercials at the Library of Congress. While this website is relatively small, it provides a good resource for studying the history of post–World War II consumer culture in terms of content and technique.

Still advertisement from *Fifty Years of Coca-Cola Television Advertisements* [236]. *(Two Contour Bottles next to Fence and Western Saddle, Ad # W6469. Permission courtesy of The Coca-Cola Company.)*

237. Freedom of Information Act, Electronic Reading Room

Federal Bureau of Investigation
http://foia.fbi.gov/room.htm

Thousands of documents from more than 150 FBI files, declassified due to Freedom of Information Act requests, are available here. No contextual information is available concerning individual documents, although file headnotes identify the person or event profiled in short one-sentence to one-paragraph descriptions. Documents, available in PDF format, have been categorized in the following manner: famous persons, historical interest, violent crime, gangster era, espionage, and "unusual phenomena" such as UFOs and animal mutilations. Many documents have been heavily censored and are barely legible. Court cases from the first half of the twentieth century include the Sacco-Vanzetti case in the 1920s; the 1932 Bonus March;

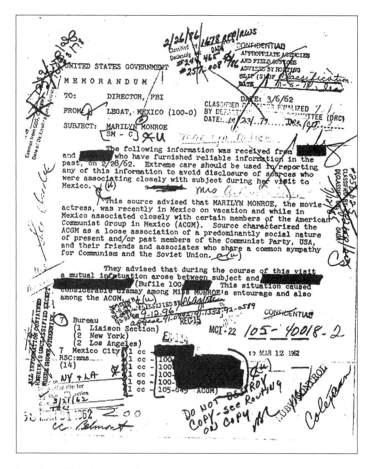

Page from FBI file on Marilyn Monroe, in *Freedom of Information Act, Electronic Reading Room* [237]. *(Electronic Reading Room, Federal Bureau of Investigation.)*

the Black Legion of the 1930s; the Young Communist League, 1939–1941; and the *Daily Worker* in the late 1940s and 1950s. More recent cases include the murder of three civil rights workers in Mississippi in 1964; SNCC, beginning in 1964; the Ku Klux Klan in 1964 and 1965; a Black Panther Party chapter beginning in 1969; the Watergate break-in of 1972; the white hate group Posse Comitas in 1973; the Weather Underground in the 1970s; and the Gay Activists Alliance of the 1970s.

238. Gulf War

Frontline, Public Broadcasting System
http://www.pbs.org/wgbh/pages/frontline/gulf/index.html

Focusing on Operation Desert Storm, these materials emphasize the perspectives of those directly involved. There are nineteen oral history interviews (up to twenty pages each) with eight "decision makers," seven commanders, two Iraqi officials, and two news analysts. "War Stories" presents the personal reminiscences of five pilots, available in text and audio. "Weapons and Technology" details ten ground, aircraft, and space weapons systems and munitions. A seven-minute video excerpt from the *Frontline* program is available as well as four fifteen-minute episodes of a BBC radio program in text and audio. The website includes a chronology, ten maps, a bibliography, facts and statistics, and brief essays on press coverage and Iraqi war deaths. Links are available to five websites produced to accompany more recent *Frontline* reports on Iraq.

239. Herblock's History: Political Cartoons from the Crash to the Millennium

Library of Congress
http://www.loc.gov/rr/print/swann/herblock/

The 150 cartoons presented here were drawn between 1929 and 2000 by three-time Pulitzer Prize–winning political cartoonist Herblock (Herbert Block). Cartoons comment on major events and public issues. The website also presents an essay by Block on "the cartoon as an opinion medium," a biographical essay, and fifteen caricatures of the cartoonist by well-known colleagues. Cartoons are organized according to thirteen chronological sections, with an additional segment devoted to presidents. Brief annotations provide historical context for each image. A tribute website by the *Washington Post*, Herblock's longtime employer, offers additional cartoons and essays by Block (http://www.washingtonpost.com/wp-srv/metro/specials/herblock/index.html).

240. Legacy Tobacco Documents Library

University of California, San Francisco Library; American Legacy Foundation
http://legacy.library.ucsf.edu

More than forty million pages from more than seven million tobacco industry documents are presented on this website. Documents were made public as a stipulation of the 1998 Master Settlement Agreement to settle multiple lawsuits. Index records, prepared by tobacco companies, can be searched by full text. Documents range from the 1930s to 2002, though most were created since the 1950s, and deal with

Cartoon, "Nixon Hanging Between the Tapes," *Washington Post*, 24 May 1974, from *Herblock's History: Political Cartoons from the Crash to the Millennium* [239]. *(A 1974 Herblock Cartoon, copyright by The Herb Block Foundation.)*

industry concerns such as marketing, sales, advertising, research and development, manufacturing, and expansion of business to developing countries. There are eighty links to related websites and promises to include more documents in the future. This project offers an abundance of material for studying the history of smoking, advertising, and twentieth-century American business practices.

241. The Living Room Candidate: Presidential Campaign Commercials, 1952–2008

American Museum of the Moving Image
http://www.livingroomcandidate.org/

This website presents more than 250 commercials that appeared on American television sets beginning in 1952 to sell presidential candidates to the public. Advertisements from each election to the present are accessible by year as well as by common themes and strategies used over time, such as "Commander in Chief," "Fear," "Children," and "Real People." Advertisements are also browsable by issue, such as civil rights, cor-

Map, 2000 presidential election, from *The Living Room Candidate: Presidential Campaign Commercials, 1952–2008* [241]. *(From the online exhibition "The Living Room Candidate: Presidential Campaign Commercials 1952–2008," Museum of the Moving Image.)*

ruption, war, taxes, and welfare. This collection includes well-known ads such as the "Daisy Ad" and well-known public figures, such as Harry Belafonte's advertisement in support of John Kennedy, as well as many others that may be less familiar in the twenty-first century. Essays focus on analyzing advertising strategies of major party candidates and a program guide presents a history of the usage of television commercials in campaigns.

242. Making the Macintosh: Technology and Culture in Silicon Valley

Alex Soojung-Kim Pang, Stanford University Library
http://library.stanford.edu/mac/

The history of the Macintosh computer is presented on this website. Rather than profile Apple Computer's leader, Steve Jobs, and well-publicized software and hardware developers, materials include thirteen interviews with designers, technical writers, Apple employees, a Berkeley user group organizer, and a San Francisco journalist who covered early developments. In addition, nearly ninety documents from the late 1970s to the present chart company and user group developments, beginning with roots in the 1960s counterculture philosophy. Documents include "From Satori to Silicon Valley," a lecture by Theodore Roszak first delivered in 1985 with afterthoughts added in 2000. There are thirteen texts by the first Mac designer, Jef Raskin; press releases and other marketing materials; and texts relating to user groups. More than one hundred images include patent drawings and product photographs.

243. Multilaterals Project

Fletcher School of Law and Diplomacy, Tufts University
http://fletcher.tufts.edu/multilaterals.html

Texts of about 300 international multilateral treaties, agreements, and conventions are available on this website, from the Treaty of Westphalia (1648) to the International

Code of Conduct on the Distribution and Use of Pesticides (November 2002). Originally designed to provide environmental agreements, this website now offers additional agreements, including drafts of many documents. Materials are arranged according to ten categories: atmosphere and space; flora and fauna, biodiversity; cultural protection; diplomatic relations; general; human rights; marine and coastal; other environmental; trade and commercial relations; and rules of warfare, arms control. Most of the texts date from the post–World War II period to the present. Listings are also arranged in chronological order and users may search by keyword. There are links to approximately 120 additional sources on treaties and conventions.

244. Oral History Digital Collection

Center for Historic Preservation, William F. Maag Jr. Library,
Youngstown State University
http://www.maag.ysu.edu/oralhistory/oral_hist.html

These full-text first-person narratives present the voices of more than 2,000 people from northeast Ohio discussing issues significant to the state and the nation. These oral histories, collected since 1974, focus on a range of topics such as ethnic culture, including African American, Greek, Irish, Italian, Jewish, Puerto Rican, Romanian, and Russian, and industry, such as steel, pottery, brick, coal, and railroads. Others discuss labor relations, including women in labor unions, wars (World War II, Vietnam War, Gulf War), college life (including the shootings by National Guard troops at Kent State in 1970), the Holocaust, and religion. Subject access is available through more than 200 topics listed alphabetically.

245. Public Papers of the Presidents of the United States, 1992–2004

National Archives and Records Administration, Office of the Federal Register
http://www.gpoaccess.gov/pubpapers/index.html

Digitized versions of twenty volumes of *Public Papers of the Presidents of the United States*, spanning from 1992 to 2004, are presented on this website. Materials include papers and speeches issued by the Office of the Press Secretary during the terms of William J. Clinton (seventeen volumes, 1993–2001), in addition to two volumes pertaining to George H. W. Bush for 1992, and four volumes for George W. Bush (January 20–June 30, 2004). The documents, including addresses, statements, letters, and interviews with the press, are compiled by the Office of the Federal Register and published in chronological order. Also included are appendices with daily schedules and meetings, nominations to the Senate, proclamations, executive orders, and photographic portfolios. Users may access multiple volumes by keyword searches and separate volumes by title of document, type, subject matter, and personal names.

246. Selling the Computer Revolution: Marketing Brochures in the Collection

Computer History Museum in Mountain View, California
http://www.computerhistory.org/brochures/index.php

Presenting more than 250 computer marketing brochures from 1948 to 1988, this collection represents materials from more than ninety companies. Visitors can explore the entire collection or browse by company. Categories include calculators, mainframes, minicomputers, personal computers, supercomputers, applications for which the computer was intended, and decade. Of particular interest are six early marketing brochures from Apple Computer, a brochure for the Commodore 64 computer, and two mid-1950s IBM brochures for "electronic data processing machines." Each group of brochures is accompanied by a brief introduction with historical information about the company, category, type of application, or decade. The full contents of each brochure are available for viewing or downloading in PDF format and each brochure is accompanied by descriptive data.

247. September 11 Digital Archive

Center for History and New Media, George Mason University
http://911digitalarchive.org/

This archive records the histories of people affected by the terrorist attacks of September 11, 2001 (9/11), including more than 150,000 stories and more than 40,000 emails from around the world. The website is constantly growing and the sources are viewable through galleries. Items include still images, including photographs, digital art, and artwork; moving images, including video files and digital animations; documents, including flyers, reports, and articles; and stories, emails, and voicemails. The supporting information is strong as well. The FAQ section includes numerous links with information about the chronology and a timeline, including flight paths and building collapses; information about hijackers, victims, and rescuers; memorials and rebuilding efforts; and the 9/11 Commission Report. Visitors are invited to submit their own recollections.

248. Teach Women's History Project

Feminist Majority Foundation
http://www.feminist.org/research/teachersguide/teach1.html

These teaching and reference materials focus on the women's rights movement of the past fifty years and its opposing forces. Teaching materials include forty primary documents selected from *The Feminist Chronicles: 1953–1993*, ranging from the first National Organization for Women (NOW) statement of purpose to topical task force statements. Twenty-eight suggestions for further reading in women's history, feminist theory, and contemporary women's issues, as well as listings for twenty relevant organizations, appear in the "Additional Resources" section. A current "Feminist Internet Gateway" provides fifteen annotated links in "History of Women/Social Studies." Additional topics ranging from arts and media to reproductive rights and their annotated links are available in the "Reviewed Links" section.

249. Vietnam Center and Archive

Vietnam Center, Texas Tech University
http://vietnam.ttu.edu/

This massive website furnishes several large collections. The "Oral History Project" presents full transcriptions of more than 475 audio oral histories conducted with U.S. men and women who served in Vietnam. The "Virtual Vietnam Archive" offers more than 408,000 pages from more than 270,000 documents regarding the Vietnam

War in addition to a number of video interviews. The website focuses on military and diplomatic history, but aims to record the experiences of ordinary individuals involved in Vietnam and on the home front. Additional items address Thailand, Laos, and Cambodia, as well as Americans and Vietnamese. Secondary and reference resources are also available, including conference papers, and video versions of a 1996 address by former ambassador William Colby on "Turning Points in the Vietnam War."

Photograph, GIs greeting Nixon, from *Vietnam Center and Archive* [249].
(Courtesy of the Vietnam Center and Archive, Texas Tech University. Number VA004674.)

Photograph, *Washington Post*, 8 August 1974, from *Watergate Revisited* [250].
(Courtesy of Magnum Photos. Photographer Alex Webb, 1974.)

250. Watergate Revisited

Washington Post

http://www.washingtonpost.com/wp-srv/politics/special/watergate/index.html

This is a thorough introduction to the Watergate scandal. Created by the *Washington Post*, the newspaper whose investigative journalism led to President Richard M. Nixon's downfall, the website provides more than eighty relevant news stories. It also offers links to twenty documents—speeches, tape transcriptions, and Nixon's letter of resignation—in the National Archives and the Nixon Library. A detailed timeline links to *Post* stories, and brief biographies introduce twenty-six "key players" in various phases of the scandal. Users may listen to eight audio clips and view eleven video clips, such as Nixon's "I am not a crook" speech, announcement of his resignation, and farewell to his staff, as well as John Dean's testimony. The *Post*'s Bob Woodward and Ben Bradlee discuss the scandal in the transcript of a 1997 interview and a video recording of a 2002 forum. The website also includes a link to twenty cartoons by the *Post*'s Herblock, photographs, and an interactive quiz.

A Glossary of Common Internet Terms

A more extensive glossary may be found at: **http://www.matisse.net/files/ glossary.html**.

Attachment: A document, photo, or other file that is sent via electronic mail. Users can download the attachment to read or view it. A writing assignment, for example, can be sent as an attachment.

Blog: (*short for* **Weblog**) A website that contains periodic, reverse chronologically ordered posts on a common webpage. Such a website is accessible to any Internet user. Individual posts (which taken together are the blog or weblog) share either a particular theme or a single or small group of authors.

Bookmark: (*also* **Favorite**) A browser function that "saves" a website's location for easy return later on.

Broadband: Refers to the method by which data are transmitted to your computer. Communication via DSL, an Ethernet line, or a cable is considered broadband, as compared to transmission over a standard telephone line, which is not. Broadband transmissions can process more data in a shorter amount of time than telephone lines.

Browser: *See* **Web Browser**.

Chat: Synchronous communication between computers on the Internet using voice, video, or plain text. Common chat interfaces include Yahoo! Messenger, IRC, AIM, and Windows Messenger.

Cookie: (*also* **HTTP Cookie**) A packet of information sent by a server to a browser and then sent back by the browser each time it accesses that server. Typically this is used to authenticate or identify a registered user. Other uses are maintaining a "shopping basket" of goods selected for purchase during a session at a website, website personalization (presenting different pages to different users), and tracking a particular user's visits to a website. Users who do not want their browsing and purchasing information collected can set their browser to prevent the use of cookies.

Database: A structured collection of records or information. There are a wide variety of databases, from simple tables stored in a single file to very large databases with millions of records, stored in rooms full of disk drives.

Dead Link: (*also* **Broken Link**) A URL or web address to a website that no longer exists.

Digital Image (**JPEG, TIFF, GIF, PNG**, etc.)**:** A representation of a two-dimensional image as a finite set of digital values, called pixels (short for "picture elements"). Typically, the pixels are stored in computer memory as a raster image or raster map, a two-dimensional array of small integers.

These values are often transmitted or stored in a compressed form (*e.g.,* images with a document type of *.jpeg, .png,* or *.gif,* etc.).

Digitize: To take something that is in a non-digital format, such as an audio-cassette recording or a photograph, and turn it into a digital format for distribution on computers or the Internet.

Domain Name: A name, usually words or a combination of letters and numbers, that identifies a specific website or set of websites on the Internet. For example, the domain name for **http://www.loc.gov/exhibits/gadd/4403 .html** is *loc.gov,* which tells you the type of organization (.gov or government in this case) as well as the organization (loc or Library of Congress).

Domain Name System (DNS): A system that stores information about host names and domain names on networks, such as the Internet. Most importantly, it provides an IP (Internet Protocol) address for each host name, and lists the mail exchange servers accepting email for each domain. The DNS forms a vital part of the Internet, because hardware requires IP addresses to perform routing, but humans use host names and domain names, for example in URLs and email addresses.

Download: To take a file that resides on a server and move it to another, usually smaller, computer via the Internet or FTP.

ejournal: A journal published on the Internet rather than in print.

email: (*short for* **Electronic Mail**) Notes, memos, and letters that can be sent from one person to another using an "email address."

email address: An electronic address in the format "username@host.domain" for sending email.

ezine: A magazine published on the Internet rather than in print.

Fair Use Doctrine: A body of law and court decisions that provides for limitations and exceptions to copyright protection in the United States. Fair use attempts to balance the interests of copyright holders with the public interest in the wider distribution and use of creative works by allowing certain limited uses that would otherwise be considered infringement of copyright.

FAQ (Frequently Asked Questions): A question-and-answer forum, usually about a particular website or its topic.

Flickr.com: A photosharing website that has become one of the largest repositories of digital photographic images in the world. Users upload hundreds of thousands of photographs each week to this Web 2.0 database.

FTP (File Transfer Protocol): A part of the Internet protocol suite that is able to transfer computer files between machines with widely different operating systems.

GIF (Graphic Interchange Format): A file format used for graphics on the Internet that allows browsers to display graphics. The *.gif* format is more appropriate for line drawings or maps because it provides more precise image definition. The *.jpg* or *.jpeg* format is preferred to the *.gif* format for color photographs because the *.gif* format allows only 256 colors.

Hit: Each occurrence of a user accessing a website. The popularity of websites is generally measured in "hits per day." "Hits," however, are not the most accurate accounting of actual visitors to a website because "hits" records every file accessed on a page. For example, if a webpage contains text and five images, a weblog will record six hits. Logs define a "visit" as all hits made by a unique computer during a half-hour period, so this is a more accurate number, but "visits" does not differentiate between a five-second and a thirty-minute visit. A third option is to count "page views," which more accurately records the number of complete pages accessed by users.

Homepage: The webpage that serves as a starting point or table of contents for a website. It can also mean a personal website in its entirety.

Host: (*also* **Server**) A computer that holds the webpage and is connected to the Internet so that other users (called "clients") can access it.

HTML (Hypertext Markup Language): The basic code in which most webpages are written.

HTTP (Hypertext Transfer Protocol): The method in which webpages are sent from the host to the user's browser.

Hyperlink: (*also* **Link**) Text that the user can click to go to another document or part of the website.

Hypertext System: A system for displaying information that contains references (called "hyperlinks") to other information on the system, and for easily publishing, updating, and searching for the information. The most well-known hypertext system is the World Wide Web.

Icon: A graphic symbol on which the user can click to go to another document or part of the website.

Instant Messenger (IM): A computer application that allows instant text communication between two or more people through a network such as the Internet. Instant messaging differs from email in that conversations happen in real time. Common IM interfaces include Yahoo! Messenger, IRC, AIM, and Windows Messenger.

Internet: A worldwide network of networks in which computers ("clients") communicate with servers ("hosts") or other computers using a variety of methods and for a variety of purposes, including accessing pages on the World Wide Web (WWW) or email.

IP (Internet Protocol) Address: A unique number used by computers to refer to each other when sending information through the Internet. This allows machines passing the information onward on behalf of the sender to know where to send it next. Converting to these numbers from the more human-readable form of domain addresses, such as "www.example.com," is done via the Domain Name System. The process of conversion is known as resolution of domain names.

Java: A computer language used widely on the Internet to make more sophisticated applications capable of producing animations, calculations, or database functions.

JPEG (Joint Photographic Experts Group): A file format that allows browsers to display graphics. The *.jpg* or *.jpeg* format is preferred to the *.gif* format for color photographs because the *.gif* format allows only 256 colors. The *.gif* format is more appropriate for line drawings or maps because it provides more precise image definition.

Keyword: Used in Internet searching, any word or set of words that is likely to appear on a website or that sums up part or all of the content of a particular website.

Link: *See* **Hyperlink**.

Listserv: An email discussion group or its mailing list.

Login: As a verb, to access a website using a login name and a password (sometimes called "logging on"). As a noun, the pseudonym used to access a website.

Mailing List: An electronic mailing list by which an electronic newsletter or website updates are sent to the email addresses of many individuals.

Malware: A type of software used by hackers to intrude on your computer without your consent, allowing them access to your stored data (including passwords) and possibly to seize control of your computer for their own purposes.

Metadata: Data about data. A good example is a library catalog card that contains data about the nature and location of a book—it is data about the information in the book. Metadata has become important on the World Wide Web because of the need to find useful information from the mass of information available.

Mirror: Websites that are exact replicas of the original website, but hosted elsewhere to prevent congestion or too many hits on one website at one time.

Modem: A device used by a computer to turn digital signals into analog signals to be sent over a phone line to another computer.

MP3: Based on MPEG technology, this is a file format for high-quality audio.

MPEG (Motion Picture Experts Group): A standard format for audio and video files frequently found on the Internet.

Netiquette: Proper and appropriate behavior on the Internet.

Netizen: An involved member of the Internet community, such as someone who has a blog or regularly posts (writes and publishes) opinions on websites.

Newsgroup: An electronic forum for discussing a particular topic where queries and responses are posted to a website.

Online: Originally meaning that someone was logged in to a particular service and thus "online," it now describes anything that resides on the Internet.

Password: A personal code used to access a computer account.

PDF (Portable Document Format): A common format for sharing formatted documents over the Internet. Users need the free Adobe Acrobat software in order to view the document.

Podcast: An audio or video recording that is converted into an *.mp3* file so that it can be downloaded and played on portable audio or video devices such as Apple's popular iPod.

Posting: A comment or article written by a user on a blog website or newsgroup.

Public Domain: The body of creative works and other knowledge—writing, artwork, music, science, inventions, and others—in which no person or organization has any proprietary interest. Such works and inventions are considered part of the public's cultural heritage, and anyone can use and build upon them without restriction.

QTVR (QuickTime Virtual Reality): A format for viewing a three-dimensional or panoramic view.

Search Engine: A function of a website that allows you to search for items on that website. Some websites, such as Altavista and Google, are search engines for many websites.

Server: A computer software application that carries out some task on behalf of users. This is usually divided into file serving, allowing users to store and access files on a common computer, and application serving, where the software runs a computer program to carry out some task for the users. The term is now also used to mean the physical computer on which the software runs.

Social Networking Websites: Websites designed to allow ways for users to interact through chatting; blogging; sharing files, images, or videos; or joining discussion groups. On popular social networking sites such as MySpace, Facebook, and Bebo, users create a profile and invite "friends" to view their profiles and interact. Some sites allow users to create groups based on shared interests and to discuss common topics.

Spider: A computer program that maps or finds all the webpages at a certain website.

Streaming Media: Audio or video that "streams" continuously through a player such as Real Audio or Windows Media Player instead of first requiring a download.

Subscription Website: A website that requires a monthly or annual contribution in order to access its content.

TCP/IP (Transmission Control Protocol/Internet Protocol): The group of universal formats by which computers transmit and receive data on the Internet.

Upload: To send a file from one, usually smaller, computer to a server or host.

URL (Uniform Resource Locator): The "address" or "location" of a website. URLs are in the form "hostname.domain," for example, **bedfordstmartins .com**, and usually preceded by *http://*.

Username: (*also* **Login Name**) A pseudonym used to login (or log on) to a website. (*See* **Login**.)

Vlog (Video Blog): A blog that is created as a video file rather than a text.

Web 2.0: Refers to second-generation Internet developments such as wikis and social networking websites, such as Flickr, MySpace, or Facebook.

Web Browser: (*also* **Browser**) A software package that enables a user to display and interact with HTML documents hosted by web servers. The largest networked collection of hypertext documents is known as the World Wide Web. Common web browsers include Internet Explorer, Netscape Navigator, Safari, and Firefox.

Weblog: *See* **Blog**.

Website: A virtual place on the World Wide Web that contains multimedia and text. Websites all have a URL that "web browsers" can use to locate them.

Wiki: Refers to software platforms that allow users to create and edit content on a website. The most popular wiki-based website is the online encyclopedia *Wikipedia:* **http://en.wikipedia.org/wiki/Main_Page**.

WWW (World Wide Web): A medium on the Internet used for multimedia and interactive electronic communication using "web browsers" such as Internet Explorer, Opera, or Netscape.

YouTube.com: A Web 2.0 community that is built around the sharing of video content. YouTube.com users upload hundreds of thousands of video files each week.

Alphabetical List of Websites Reviewed

Numbers refer to the website entry numbers, not page numbers.

Index

Types of primary sources are listed in *italics*.
Numbers refer to the website entry numbers, not page numbers.